Comforts
of Home
Cooking

Meredith ® Books
Des Moines, Iowa

Better Homes and Gardens® Books
An imprint of Meredith® Books

Comforts of Home Cooking
Editor: Jan Miller
Contributing Editors: Diana McMillen, Carrie Mills, Winifred Moranville
Associate Art Director: Mick Schnepf
Contributing Designer: Lyne Neymeyer
Copy Chief: Terri Fredrickson
Copy and Production Editor: Victoria Forlini
Editorial Operations Manager: Karen Schirm
Managers, Book Production: Pam Kvitne, Marjorie J. Schenkelberg
Contributing Copy Editor: Donna Segal
Contributing Proofreaders: Emmy Clausing, Gretchen Kauffman, Susan J. Kling
Indexer: Elizabeth T. Parson
Electronic Production Coordinator: Paula Forest
Editorial and Design Assistants: Karen McFadden, Mary Lee Gavin
Test Kitchen Director: Lynn Blanchard
Test Kitchen Product Supervisor: Colleen Weeden

Meredith® Books
Publisher and Editor in Chief: James D. Blume
Design Director: Matt Strelecki
Managing Editor: Gregory H. Kayko
Executive Editor, Food and Crafts: Jennifer Dorland Darling

Director, Operations: George A. Susral
Director, Production: Douglas M. Johnston

Vice President and General Manager: Douglas J. Guendel

Meredith Publishing Group
President, Publishing Group: Stephen M. Lacy
Vice President-Publishing Director: Bob Mate

Meredith Corporation
Chairman and Chief Executive Officer: William T. Kerr

Chairman of the Executive Committee: E. T. Meredith III

Our seal assures you that every recipe in *Comforts of Home Cooking* has been tested in the Better Homes and Gardens® Test Kitchen. This means that each recipe is practical and reliable, and meets our high standards of taste appeal. We guarantee your satisfaction with this book for as long as you own it.

All of us at Better Homes and Gardens® Books are dedicated to providing you with the information and ideas you need to create delicious foods. We welcome your comments and suggestions. Write to us at: Better Homes and Gardens Books, Cookbook Editorial Department, 1716 Locust St., Des Moines, IA 50309-3023.

If you would like to purchase any of our cooking, crafts, gardening, home improvement, or home decorating and design books, check wherever quality books are sold. Or visit us at: bhgbooks.com
For more recipes, visit our Recipe Center at www.bhg.com

Food is a celebration of one of life's joys and a link to our heritage...

Good food is a passion with Midwesterners. They love preparing and passing along their favorite recipes that we regularly share with you on the pages of *Midwest Living* magazine. In *Comforts of Home Cooking* we team up with the food editors of *Better Homes and Gardens* Books to showcase the Heartland's diverse flavors, from recipes selected by a farm cook to an exquisitely prepared meal at a gourmet restaurant. Our focus—and the source of our inspiration—is always real people from real places. Now you can bring these great flavors into your own kitchen with *Comforts of Home Cooking*—your friends and family are sure to follow. So, pull up a chair and enjoy the company, the conversation and the satisfaction of sharing one of life's greatest passions with those you love. 🌿

Diana McMillen, Senior Food Editor

Midwest Living magazine

Learn more about *Midwest Living* magazine at midwestliving.com

Cranberry Chocolate Layer Cake, page 184

contents

Some things are meant to be shared—

and good food is one of them, whether a

casual dinner on the deck with friends

or a warm slice of banana bread savored

Good Food,
Good Friends

over coffee with a neighbor. Turn to

these company-worthy recipes to create

meals sure to bring rave reviews.

Lynn's Herb and Garlic Pork, page 30

Orange Biscuit Coffee Rolls

MAKES 10 SERVINGS (20 BISCUITS).

Paula Morris, backyard gardener extraordinaire from Grosse Pointe Park, Michigan, shares her recipe for gooey pull-apart rolls. So easy and so good, her recipe starts with two packages of refrigerated biscuits. It's ready to pop in the oven in 15 minutes.

1¼   cups sugar
1   tablespoon finely shredded
      orange peel
⅓   cup orange juice
¼   cup butter, melted
2   10-ounce packages refrigerated
      biscuits (10 biscuits each)
      Orange peel strips (optional)
      Fresh herb sprigs (optional)

Prep: 15 minutes Bake: 30 minutes
Cool: 30 minutes Oven: 375°F
Nutrition facts per serving: 240 cal., 6 g fat,
13 mg chol., 410 mg sodium, 44 g carbo.,
0 g fiber, 3 g pro.

1. Grease a 10-inch fluted tube pan. Set aside.

2. In a small bowl, combine sugar and orange peel (be sure to break up any orange peel clumps). In another small bowl, combine orange juice and melted butter.

3. Separate biscuits. Dip each into the orange juice-butter mixture; roll in the sugar–orange peel mixture.

4. In the prepared pan, arrange the biscuits upright with flat sides together. Pour any remaining orange juice-butter mixture over biscuits. Bake in a 375° oven for 30 minutes. Cool in pan on a wire rack for 1 minute. Turn pan upside down on a serving plate. Remove the pan. Cool for 30 to 45 minutes. Serve warm. Garnish center of ring with orange peel strips and fresh herbs, if you like.

Easy Banana-Nut Loaves

MAKES 2 LOAVES (32 SERVINGS).

Two for one! *This nut-filled banana bread recipe makes two loaves. Keep one and share the other with a neighbor. Or tuck the extra loaf in your freezer—it keeps for up to a month. Pull it out when unexpected guests show up at your front door.*

2 cups self-rising flour*
1 cup packed light brown sugar
1 cup mashed ripe bananas
    (2 to 3 medium)
½ cup butter, softened
3 tablespoons milk
2 eggs
1 cup chopped walnuts, toasted

Prep: 15 minutes Bake: 45 minutes Oven: 350°F
Nutrition facts per serving: 108 cal., 6 g fat,
22 mg chol., 137 mg sodium, 13 g carbo.,
1 g fiber, 2 g pro.

1. Grease two 8×4×2-inch loaf pans; set aside. In a large mixing bowl, combine 1 cup of the self-rising flour* and the brown sugar. Add mashed ripe bananas, butter and milk. Beat with an electric mixer on low speed until combined. Beat on high speed for 2 minutes.

2. Add eggs and the remaining flour. Beat until blended. Stir in walnuts.

3. Pour into prepared loaf pans. Bake in a 350° oven for 45 to 50 minutes or until a wooden toothpick inserted near the centers comes out clean. Cool 10 minutes. Remove from pans; cool thoroughly on wire racks. Wrap and store overnight for easier slicing.

Test Kitchen Tip: If you prefer to substitute all-purpose flour for the self-rising flour, use 2 cups all-purpose flour, 2 teaspoons baking powder, ½ teaspoon baking soda and ¼ teaspoon salt in place of the 2 cups self-rising flour.

Devonshire Splits

MAKES 20 SPLITS.

Fill these sweet little yeast buns with strawberry preserves and a cream mixture. If you serve them with a pot of tea in England, the event is known as a cream tea. No matter how you serve them, they are certain to be a hit.

1	package active dry yeast
1	teaspoon granulated sugar
¼	cup warm milk (110°F to 115°F)
4	to 4½ cups all-purpose flour
¾	cup milk
½	cup butter
⅓	cup granulated sugar
½	teaspoon salt
	Strawberry preserves
	Devon Cream or purchased lemon curd
	Sifted powdered sugar (optional)

Prep: 40 minutes Rise: 2 hours 15 minutes
Bake: 12 minutes Cool: 1 hour Oven: 375°F
Nutrition facts per split: 258 cal.,
10 g fat, 28 mg chol., 156 mg sodium,
38 g carbo., 1 g fiber, 4 g pro.

1. In a small bowl, dissolve yeast and the 1 teaspoon sugar in the ¼ cup warm milk. Set the mixture aside for 5 to 10 minutes or until foamy.

2. Place 2 cups of the flour in a large mixing bowl. In a small saucepan, heat and stir the ¾ cup milk, butter, ⅓ cup sugar and salt until warm (120° to 130°) and butter almost melts. Add milk mixture to flour in mixing bowl. Add yeast mixture. Beat with an electric mixer on low to medium speed for 30 seconds, scraping bowl. Beat on high speed for 3 minutes. Using a wooden spoon, stir in as much of the remaining flour as you can.

3. Turn dough out onto a lightly floured surface. Knead in enough of the remaining flour to make a moderately soft dough that is smooth and elastic (3 to 5 minutes total). Shape dough into a ball. Place in a lightly greased bowl, turning once to grease surface of dough. Cover and let rise in warm place until double (about 1½ hours).

4. Punch dough down. Turn dough out onto a lightly floured surface. Cover and let rest 10 minutes. Divide dough into 20 portions. Shape portions into small balls. Place balls 2 inches apart on greased baking sheets. Using your fingers, slightly flatten to circles 3 inches in diameter. Cover; let rise until nearly doubled (45 to 60 minutes).

5. Bake in a 375° oven for 12 to 15 minutes or until buns are golden brown. Immediately remove buns from baking sheets. Cool on wire rack.

6. To serve, slice each bun in half crosswise. Spread each bottom half with about 1 tablespoon strawberry preserves; top with about 1 tablespoon Devon Cream or lemon curd. Place each bun top over filling. Sprinkle with powdered sugar, if you like.

Devon Cream: In a small bowl, combine one 8-ounce package cream cheese, softened, ⅓ cup dairy sour cream and 1 tablespoon granulated sugar. Beat until smooth. Makes 1½ cups.

Savory Cheese Scones

MAKES 8 TO 10 SCONES.

Traditionally scones are eaten at breakfast or tea, but Linda Finger's savory scones flavored with sage, dry mustard and a pinch of ground red pepper for zip are a hearty accompaniment for a main-dish salad or a steamy bowl of soup.

2	cups self-rising flour*
2	tablespoons sugar
1	teaspoon snipped fresh sage (optional)
½	teaspoon dry mustard (optional)
⅛	teaspoon ground red pepper
3	tablespoons butter
¾	cup shredded sharp cheddar, Cheshire or Wensleydale cheese
1	beaten egg
6	tablespoons half-and-half, light cream or milk
1	egg
1	tablespoon water

Prep: 20 minutes Bake: 8 minutes
Cool: 5 minutes Oven: 425°F
Nutrition facts per scone: 239 cal., 11 g fat, 81 mg chol., 529 mg sodium, 27 g carbo., 1 g fiber, 8 g pro.

1. In a medium mixing bowl, stir together self-rising flour*, sugar, sage (if you like), mustard (if you like) and red pepper. Using a pastry blender, cut in butter until mixture resembles coarse crumbs. Stir in cheese. Make a well in the center of the flour mixture.

2. In a small bowl, combine the 1 beaten egg and the half-and-half. Add egg mixture all at once to flour mixture. Using a fork, stir until just moistened.

3. Turn the dough out onto a lightly floured surface. Quickly knead by gently folding and pressing dough for 10 to 12 strokes or until nearly smooth. Pat or lightly roll dough to ½ inch thick. Cut the dough with a floured 2½-inch round biscuit cutter.

4. Place scones 1 inch apart on an ungreased large baking sheet. In a small bowl, stir together the 1 remaining egg and water. Lightly brush tops of scones with the egg mixture. Bake in a 425° oven for 8 to 10 minutes or until golden. Remove scones from baking sheet and cool on wire racks for 5 minutes. Serve warm with butter, if you like.

*__Test Kitchen Tip:__ If you prefer to substitute all-purpose flour for the self-rising flour, use 2 cups all-purpose flour, 2 teaspoons baking powder, ½ teaspoon baking soda and ¼ teaspoon salt in place of the 2 cups self-rising flour.

Bread Machine
Sesame Breadsticks

MAKES 40 BREADSTICKS.

Let your bread machine, an excellent kitchen helper, do the mixing; you shape the dough. A sesame seed coating adds flavor and crunch to this meal mate. For variety sprinkle breadsticks with poppy seeds, cracked black pepper or grated Parmesan cheese.

1	cup water
½	cup cracked wheat
1	cup fat-free milk
2	tablespoons olive oil or canola oil
2	cups bread flour
2	cups whole wheat flour
2	teaspoons brown sugar
1	teaspoon salt
1½	teaspoons active dry yeast or bread machine yeast
1	slightly beaten egg white
1	tablespoon water
	Sesame seeds

Prep: 30 minutes Bake: 15 minutes Oven: 350°F
Nutrition facts per breadstick: 63 cal., 1 g fat, 0 mg chol., 64 mg sodium, 12 g carbo., 1 g fiber, 2 g pro.

1. In a small saucepan, bring the 1 cup water to boiling; remove from heat. Stir in cracked wheat. Let stand for 3 minutes; drain well. Stir milk into the cracked wheat.

2. Add the cracked wheat mixture, oil, flours, brown sugar, salt and yeast to a bread machine according to the manufacturer's directions. Select the dough cycle. When the cycle is complete, remove the dough from machine. Punch down. Cover and let rest for 10 minutes.

3. Divide dough in half. On a lightly floured surface, roll each portion of dough into a 10×8-inch rectangle. In a small bowl, combine egg white and the 1 tablespoon water. Brush dough with the egg white mixture; sprinkle with sesame seeds. Cut each rectangle crosswise into twenty ½-inch-wide strips.

4. Twist and gently stretch each strip until it's 10 inches long. Place the strips on greased baking sheets. Press ends down.

5. Bake strips in a 350° oven for 15 minutes or until golden brown. Remove breadsticks from baking sheets. Cool on wire racks.

Test Kitchen Tip: To store, cool breadsticks; place in airtight freezer container or self-sealing plastic freezer bag. Seal, label and freeze for up to 2 months.

Easy Aïoli

MAKES ⅔ CUP, 10 (1-TABLESPOON) SERVINGS.

Eight-year-old Cecilia Goff likes whisking the olive oil for the aïoli (garlic mayonnaise) when she cooks with her dad, Ken Goff, executive chef at Dakota Restaurant in Saint Paul. She's especially good at arranging items on the platter to be dipped in the aïoli.

⅓ cup mayonnaise

1 to 3 cloves garlic, minced

1 teaspoon water

½ teaspoon lemon juice

⅛ teaspoon kosher salt or coarse sea salt

¼ to ⅓ cup extra-virgin olive oil

Start to Finish: 10 minutes

Nutrition facts per 1 tablespoon serving:
92 cal., 10 g fat, 2 mg chol., 58 mg sodium,
0 g carbo., 0 g fiber, 0 g pro.

1. In a medium bowl, combine the mayonnaise and garlic. Whisk in the water, lemon juice and salt until the mixture is smooth. Slowly whisk in the olive oil, a few teaspoons at a time, until the mixture reaches the thickness you like. (If the mixture becomes too thick, whisk in additional water to reach the desired consistency.)

2. Serve as a sauce with hot or chilled vegetables, cooked and chilled shellfish or chilled leftover beef and lamb.

Basil Aïoli: Stir 2 teaspoons of snipped fresh basil into prepared Aïoli.

Kent's Hot-Off-The-Grill Potatoes

MAKES 4 SERVINGS.

Test Kitchen home economist Colleen Weeden knows her way around the kitchen but defers to her husband, Kent, when it comes to cooking potatoes. He says the only way to cook them is on the grill. His secret: split them so they don't take so long to cook.

4 medium potatoes
4 tablespoons butter
  Seasoned pepper or your
    favorite seasoning blend
  Dried parsley

Prep: 20 minutes Grill: 1 hour
Nutrition facts per serving: 275 cal.,
12 g fat, 33 mg chol., 140 mg sodium,
38 g carbo., 4 g fiber, 5 g pro.

1. Make a lengthwise cut into each potato, leaving the opposite side attached, and spread each potato apart slightly, like opening a book. Place 1 tablespoon of butter in each potato opening. Sprinkle with seasoning and parsley.

2. Wrap each potato in heavy foil. Grill on the rack of an uncovered grill directly over medium coals for 1 hour or until tender, turning occasionally.

Colleen's Easy Balsamic Chicken

MAKES 4 SERVINGS.

Colleen Weeden's simple chicken dish is perfect for a summertime gathering. With preparation out of the way, enjoy appetizers with your guests as the chicken marinates. For ensured success, use an instant-read thermometer to check the chicken's doneness.

4	skinless, boneless chicken breast halves (about 1 pound total)
¼	cup balsamic vinegar
¼	cup olive oil
3	cloves garlic, minced
¼	teaspoon salt
¼	teaspoon crushed red pepper

Prep: 15 minutes Marinate: 1 hour
Grill: 10 minutes

Nutrition facts per serving: 177 cal., 6 g fat, 66 mg chol., 125 mg sodium, 2 g carbo., 0 g fiber, 26 g pro.

1. Place each chicken breast between two pieces of plastic wrap. Pound each lightly with the flat side of a meat mallet to make an even thickness (about ½ inch). Remove plastic wrap.

2. Place the chicken in a self-sealing plastic bag set in a shallow dish. In a small bowl or small glass measure, stir together balsamic vinegar, olive oil, garlic, salt and pepper. Pour over chicken; seal bag. Marinate in the refrigerator for 1 to 4 hours, turning bag occasionally.

3. Drain chicken, reserving marinade. Place chicken on the rack of an uncovered grill directly over medium coals. Grill, uncovered, for 10 to 12 minutes or until an instant-read thermometer registers 170°, turning once halfway through grilling time and brushing with marinade. Discard any remaining marinade.

Hot Sauce and Cola Chicken Wings

MAKES 12 APPETIZER SERVINGS OR 4 TO 6 MAIN-DISH SERVINGS.

Though they make an unlikely pair for an easy chicken wing marinade, bottled hot pepper sauce and bubbling cola give a sweet hotness to this appetizer. A spoonful of the Avocado Salsa makes a refreshing accompaniment.

24	chicken wings (about 4½ pounds total), tips removed
1	12-ounce can cola
1	2-ounce bottle hot pepper sauce
2	tablespoons olive oil
3	cloves garlic, minced
¼	cup cola
1	tablespoon unsalted butter
	Avocado Salsa
	Fresh lime halves (optional)
	Crushed red pepper (optional)
	Scented geranium leaves (optional)
	Small pequin chile peppers (optional)

Prep: 20 minutes Marinate: 5 hours
Roast: 20 minutes Oven: 450°F
Nutrition facts per appetizer serving:
212 cal., 17 g fat, 60 mg chol., 90 mg sodium, 5 g carbo., 2 g fiber, 10 g pro.

1. Place the chicken wings in a large self-sealing plastic bag set in a shallow dish. Pour the 12-ounce can of cola over the chicken wings. Seal bag. Marinate in the refrigerator for at least 1 hour or for up to 4 hours, turning bag occasionally. Drain the chicken wings, discarding the cola marinade. Return wings to bag; pour the hot pepper sauce over the chicken wings. Close bag. Marinate in the refrigerator for 4 to 24 hours, turning bag occasionally. Drain the chicken wings, discarding the hot pepper sauce marinade.

2. In a very large skillet, heat the oil over medium-high heat. Cook 12 chicken wings in the hot oil over medium heat until brown on all sides. Remove from skillet; place in a well-greased, foil-lined large roasting pan. Repeat with remaining chicken wings, adding more oil, if necessary. Reserve the pan drippings. Bake wings in a 450° oven for 20 minutes or until tender and no longer pink.

3. For sauce: In the same skillet, cook and stir garlic in pan drippings over medium heat for 1 minute. Add the ¼ cup cola. Bring to boiling; reduce heat. Simmer, stirring occasionally, for 1 minute or until liquid is reduced to about 2 tablespoons. Whisk in butter until melted and the sauce is thickened. Keep warm.

4. To serve, spoon Avocado Salsa into the center of 4 to 6 dinner plates. Place chicken wings around the salsa. Drizzle the warm sauce over chicken wings. If you like, serve with lime halves sprinkled with crushed red pepper and garnish with scented geranium leaves and small pequin chile peppers.

Avocado Salsa: In a medium bowl, combine 2 medium avocados, halved, seeded, peeled and finely chopped; 1 large tomato, finely chopped; 4 green onions, finely chopped; ¼ cup snipped fresh cilantro; 3 tablespoons rice vinegar; 2 tablespoons lime juice; 2 cloves garlic, minced; ¼ to ½ teaspoon crushed red pepper and ⅛ teaspoon salt. Cover and chill for 1 to 2 hours. Makes about 2½ cups salsa.

Chicken Drumsticks Extraordinaire

MAKES 4 SERVINGS.

"Drumsticks are one of those kid-friendly ingredients," Food Editor Diana McMillen says. She likes to brush them with a pestolike mixture made with aromatic fresh basil and pecans. If the kids seem pickier than usual, brush it on sparingly.

1	cup lightly packed fresh basil leaves
½	cup broken pecans
¼	cup olive oil
2	cloves garlic, minced
¼	teaspoon salt
¼	teaspoon black pepper
8	meaty chicken drumsticks

Prep: 20 minutes Grill: 35 minutes
Nutrition facts per serving without skin:
406 cal., 29 g fat, 122 mg chol., 258 mg sodium, 3 g carbo., 2 g fiber, 34 g pro.

1. In a blender container or small food processor bowl, combine the basil, pecans, olive oil, garlic, salt and pepper. Cover and blend or process until pureed, scraping down sides as needed.

2. Remove the skin from the chicken, if you like. Place chicken on the rack of uncovered grill directly over medium coals. Brush chicken with about half of the basil mixture. Grill, uncovered, for 35 to 45 minutes or until an instant-read thermometer registers 180°, turning once halfway through grilling time and brushing with the remaining basil mixture. (Watch carefully for flare-ups after turning chicken. Move chicken to a different area of the grill until the flare-up ends.)

Nutrition Note: Trim fat per serving by removing the skin from chicken legs before brushing with the basil mixture.

Deb's Spicy Moroccan Glazed Chicken

MAKES 4 SERVINGS.

"I've used this glaze recipe for years and only over chicken," Garden Editor Deb Wiley says. *"I often serve it with a green vegetable such as asparagus or broccoli and curried couscous mixed with raisins and carrots."*

4	medium skinless, boneless chicken breast halves (about 1 pound total)
½	cup plain yogurt
⅓	cup lime juice
2	tablespoons olive oil
2	tablespoons honey
2	cloves garlic, minced
1	teaspoon bottled hot pepper sauce
½	teaspoon ground turmeric
½	teaspoon ground cardamom
½	teaspoon ground allspice
½	teaspoon ground cumin
¼	teaspoon salt
¼	teaspoon ground white pepper

Prep: 15 minutes Marinate: 4 hours
Grill: 12 minutes
Nutrition facts per serving: 191 cal., 6 g fat, 67 mg chol., 150 mg sodium, 7 g carbo., 0 g fiber, 27 g pro.

1. Place chicken in a large self-sealing plastic bag set in a shallow bowl.

2. Combine remaining ingredients and pour over chicken, turning chicken to coat. Seal bag and marinate in the refrigerator for 4 to 8 hours.

3. Drain chicken, reserving marinade. Place chicken on the rack of an uncovered grill directly over medium coals. Grill, uncovered, for 12 to 15 minutes or until the chicken is no longer pink and an instant-read thermometer registers 170°, turning once halfway through grilling time and brushing with marinade. Discard any remaining marinade.

Charlie's Margarita Kabobs

MAKES 6 SERVINGS.

Food stylist Charles Worthington creates beautiful food to photograph and tantalizing recipes to taste. He makes this tangy kabob with a brushing sauce based on the classic cocktail. The alcohol helps the flavors blend subtly, but you can omit it.

1¼   pounds fresh or frozen jumbo shrimp in shells and/or skinless, boneless chicken breasts or thighs

1   large red or green sweet pepper, cut into bite-size pieces

1   medium red onion, cut into wedges

1   cup orange marmalade

⅓   cup lime juice

¼   cup tequila (optional)

2   tablespoons cooking oil

2   tablespoons snipped fresh cilantro

2   cloves garlic, minced

6   ½-inch slices peeled, fresh pineapple

Prep: 30 minutes Grill: 10 minutes
Nutrition facts per serving: 289 cal., 15 g fat, 108 mg chol., 137 mg sodium, 47 g carbo., 4 g fiber, 15 g pro.

1. Thaw shrimp, if frozen. Peel and devein shrimp, leaving tails intact. Rinse shrimp and pat dry. For chicken, cut into 1-inch pieces. Thread shrimp and/or chicken, sweet pepper and onion onto six 10- to 12-inch skewers.

2. In a small saucepan, combine marmalade, lime juice, tequila (if you like), oil, cilantro and garlic. Cook and stir just until marmalade melts. Divide in half.

3. Grill kabobs on a greased rack of an uncovered grill directly over medium coals for 10 to 12 minutes or until shrimp turn opaque and chicken is no longer pink, turning once.

4. During the last 5 minutes of grilling, add pineapple to grill rack and brush kabobs and pineapple with half of the sauce mixture. Turn pineapple once. Pass remaining half of sauce with kabobs and pineapple.

Roasted Sweet and Spicy Salmon

MAKES 4 SERVINGS.

Marinated first in pineapple and lemon juice, then coated with a spicy rub, this two-step treatment doubles the flavor in every bite of salmon. Don't skip either step. Short on time? Stir together the spice rub ingredients (except for the lemon peel) the night before.

4	6-ounce fresh or frozen salmon steaks, cut 1 inch thick
¼	cup unsweetened pineapple juice
2	tablespoons lemon juice
1	tablespoon snipped fresh thyme or 1 teaspoon dried thyme, crushed
2	tablespoons brown sugar
1	tablespoon chili powder
2	teaspoons finely shredded lemon peel
1	teaspoon ground cinnamon
½	teaspoon salt
¼	teaspoon ground nutmeg or ground cardamom
	Nonstick cooking spray
	Lemon wedges (optional)

Prep: 10 minutes Marinate: 1 to 2 hours
Roast: 18 minutes   Oven: 450°F
Nutrition facts per serving: 321 cal.,
15 g fat, 105 mg chol., 393 mg sodium,
9 g carbo., 1 g fiber, 37 g pro.

1. Thaw fish, if frozen. Rinse; pat dry with paper towels. Place fish in a self-sealing plastic bag set in a shallow dish; set aside.

2. For marinade: In a small bowl, stir together pineapple juice, lemon juice and thyme. Pour over fish. Seal bag and marinate in the refrigerator for 1 to 2 hours, turning bag occasionally.

3. For dry spice rub: In a small bowl, stir together brown sugar, chili powder, lemon peel, cinnamon, salt and nutmeg.

4. Drain fish; discard marinade. Sprinkle spice rub evenly over salmon steaks; rub in with your fingers.

5. Place a wire rack in a large, shallow baking pan lined with foil; lightly coat the rack with cooking spray. Place the fish steaks on the prepared rack in the baking pan. Roast in a 450° oven for 18 to 22 minutes or until fish flakes easily when tested with a fork. Serve with lemon wedges, if you like.

Linda's Glorious Glazed Salmon

MAKES 4 SERVINGS.

Editor Linda Kast discovered this marinade for salmon on a trip to Seattle. She toyed with the ingredients at home until she came up with this version. She likes how the sweet tamari sauce gives the fish a caramelized finish.

4   fresh or frozen skinless,
    boneless salmon fillets
    (6 ounces each)
½   cup balsamic vinegar
1   tablespoon brown sugar or
    full-flavored molasses
1   teaspoon tamari sauce or
    soy sauce
¼   teaspoon finely chopped fresh
    ginger or ⅛ teaspoon
    ground ginger

Prep: 15 minutes Cook: 5 minutes
Grill: 4 minutes/½-inch thickness of fish
Nutrition facts per serving: 336 cal.,
15 g fat, 105 mg chol., 171 mg sodium,
11 g carbo., 0 g fiber, 36 g pro.

1. Thaw fish, if frozen. Rinse; pat dry with paper towels. Set fish aside. In a small saucepan, bring vinegar to boiling over medium heat. Boil gently, uncovered, about 5 minutes or until reduced by half.

2. Stir in brown sugar, tamari and ginger.

3. Brush mixture on salmon fillets. Place fish on the rack of an uncovered grill directly over medium coals. Grill for 4 to 6 minutes per ½-inch thickness or until fish flakes easily when tested with a fork, turning and brushing with tamari mixture halfway through cooking. Serve with rice pilaf and asparagus spears, if you like.

Dijon Pork

MAKES 4 SERVINGS.

Lean pork chops draped with a creamy mustard sauce are incredibly simple to prepare and deceptively rich tasting. Serve the chops with hot cooked rice or noodles to soak up every drop of the sauce.

4	boneless pork loin chops, cut ½ inch thick (about 1 pound total)
¼	teaspoon freshly ground black pepper
	Nonstick cooking spray
⅓	cup reduced-sodium chicken broth
⅓	cup fat-free half-and-half or evaporated fat-free milk
1½	to 2 tablespoons Dijon-style mustard, spicy brown mustard or honey mustard

Prep: 10 minutes Cook: 13 minutes
Nutrition facts per serving: 178 cal., 6 g fat, 62 mg chol., 149 mg sodium, 3 g carbo., 0 g fiber, 26 g pro.

1. Trim fat from pork chops. Sprinkle both sides with pepper. Lightly coat an unheated large skillet with cooking spray. Preheat over medium heat. Add pork chops; cook for 4 minutes. Turn chops; cook 4 to 6 minutes more or until pork is brown and juices run clear and an instant-read thermometer inserted in centers of chops registers 160°. Remove pork from skillet and keep warm.

2. For sauce: Add the chicken broth to skillet, stirring to loosen browned bits. Stir in half-and-half and mustard. Bring to boiling; reduce heat. Cook, uncovered, 5 to 7 minutes or until sauce is slightly thickened, stirring often.

3. To serve, transfer pork chops to a warm serving platter. Spoon sauce over pork.

Wisconsin Pork and Apples

MAKES 8 SERVINGS.

A fresh herb marinade adds the touch of a garden to the hearty marriage of pork and apples. Your family or guests will be impressed with this savory dish. You'll be amazed at what little effort it requires. The results are fork-tender and juicy.

2	tablespoons balsamic vinegar
2	tablespoons dry sherry (optional)
1	tablespoon cracked black pepper
1	tablespoon olive oil
1	tablespoon soy sauce
2	3-inch sprigs fresh rosemary
2	3-inch sprigs fresh marjoram
2	3-inch sprigs fresh thyme
2	cloves garlic, minced
2	¾-pound pork tenderloins
2	tablespoons cooking oil
	Salt
2	tablespoons unsalted butter
4	medium Gala, Golden Delicious or other cooking apples, cored and cut crosswise into ¼-inch rings
1	3-inch sprig fresh sage
¼	cup bourbon or apple juice
2	tablespoons honey

Prep: 15 minutes Marinate: 2 to 4 hours
Roast: 25 minutes Stand: 15 minutes Oven: 425°F
Nutrition facts per serving: 232 cal., 8 g fat,
63 mg chol., 187 mg sodium, 15 g carbo.,
2 g fiber, 18 g pro.

1. For marinade: In a small bowl, stir together vinegar, sherry (if you like), cracked pepper, olive oil, soy sauce, rosemary, marjoram, thyme and garlic. Place tenderloins in a large self-sealing plastic bag set in a shallow dish. Pour marinade over tenderloins. Close bag. Marinate in the refrigerator for 2 to 4 hours, turning bag occasionally.

2. Remove tenderloins from marinade, reserving marinade. In a large skillet, heat the 2 tablespoons cooking oil over medium-high heat. Sprinkle meat lightly with salt. Brown tenderloins quickly on all sides in hot oil (about 5 minutes).

3. Place tenderloins in a shallow roasting pan. Pour reserved marinade over meat. Insert a meat thermometer into the center of one of the tenderloins. Roast, uncovered, in a 425° oven for 15 minutes. Spoon pan juices over the tenderloins. Roast for 10 to 15 minutes more or until thermometer registers 160°.

4. Transfer tenderloins to a serving platter, reserving pan juices. Strain juices; set aside and keep warm. Cover tenderloins with foil and let stand for 15 minutes before carving.

5. Meanwhile, in the same large skillet, melt butter over medium heat. Add apple rings and sage sprig. Cook, uncovered, about 5 minutes or until the apples are lightly brown, stirring occasionally. Remove skillet from heat.

6. Carefully add bourbon and honey. Bring to boiling; reduce heat. Simmer, uncovered, about 5 minutes more or until apples are just tender, stirring gently and spooning bourbon mixture over apples occasionally. Discard sage sprig.

7. To serve, cut tenderloins crosswise into 1-inch slices. Arrange apple rings around sliced pork. Pour reserved pan juices over sliced pork and apples. Serve immediately.

Mom's Best Double-Meat Dinner

MAKES 8 TO 10 SERVINGS.

Serving two kinds of meat makes sense when 14 kids pack the dinner table. Betty Braun of Davenport, Iowa, remembers her mom, Patricia, putting together this roasted meat and vegetable main dish and letting the kids help while she finished up the gravy.

1	1½- to 2-pound boneless beef chuck eye roast
1	1½- to 2-pound boneless pork top loin roast
1	tablespoon cooking oil
½	teaspoon salt
½	teaspoon black pepper
1½	cups water
2½	pounds new potatoes
1½	pounds baby carrots with tops or 1½ pounds baby carrots
1	pound boiling onions, peeled
¼	cup all-purpose flour
½	cup cold water
	Salt and black pepper

Prep: 35 minutes Roast: 2 hours Oven: 350°F
Nutrition facts per serving: 369 cal.,
14 g fat, 81 mg chol., 217 mg sodium,
28 g carbo., 4 g fiber, 32 g pro.

1. In an 8-quart Dutch oven or kettle, brown meat, one piece at a time, on all sides in the hot oil. Drain off the fat. Return both pieces of the meat to the Dutch oven. Sprinkle with ½ teaspoon salt and ½ teaspoon pepper. Add 1½ cups water.

2. Cover and roast in a 350° oven for 1 hour. Meanwhile, peel a strip around each potato, if you like. If using baby carrots with tops, trim carrot tops to 1-inch; peel or scrub carrots. Add potatoes, carrots and onions to meat. Cover and roast for 1 hour or until meat and vegetables are tender. Transfer meat and vegetables to a serving platter; cover to keep warm.

3. For gravy: Measure pan drippings, scraping up the browned bits from the bottom of the pan. Add water, if needed, to make 1½ cups of liquid.

4. In the Dutch oven, whisk together flour and the ½ cup cold water. Add pan drippings. Cook and stir until thickened and bubbly. Cook and stir for 1 minute more. Serve gravy with meat and vegetables. Season meat and vegetables to taste with salt and pepper.

Lynn's Herb and Garlic Pork

MAKES 12 SERVINGS.

"I like the flavor that grilled food takes on," says Test Kitchen Director Lynn Blanchard. "It's easy to grill once you learn the technique; cleanup is simple and it doesn't heat up the house in the summer." She prepares her pork roast with garlic and herbs from her garden.

¼	cup olive oil
6	cloves garlic, minced
2	tablespoons snipped fresh basil
2	tablespoons snipped chives or chopped green onion
2	teaspoons chili powder or ¼ teaspoon ground red pepper
1	teaspoon snipped fresh sage or oregano
1	teaspoon salt
½	teaspoon black pepper
1	3- to 4-pound boneless pork top loin roast (double loin, tied)

Prep: 10 minutes Marinate: 2 hours
Grill: 1½ hours Stand: 15 minutes
Nutrition facts per serving: 181 cal., 8 g fat, 62 mg chol., 239 mg sodium, 1 g carbo., 0 g fiber, 25 g pro.

1. In a small bowl, combine all the ingredients except the meat. Place meat in a large self-sealing plastic bag set in a shallow dish. Pour marinade over meat. Seal bag and marinate in the refrigerator for 2 to 24 hours, turning the bag occasionally.

2. Remove meat from bag. Discard marinade. Insert a meat thermometer into the thickest part of the roast. (Or use an instant-read thermometer to start checking the roast after 1 hour of grilling.)

3. In a covered grill, arrange preheated coals around a drip pan (or follow manufacturer's directions for cooking over indirect heat on your gas grill). Test for medium-low heat above the pan*. Place meat on the grill rack over the drip pan. Cover and grill for 1½ to 2¼ hours or until a meat thermometer registers 155°. Remove roast from the grill and cover with foil. Let stand for 15 minutes before carving. (The meat's temperature should rise 5° upon standing to 160°.)

4. To serve, remove the strings from the roast and slice the meat. Use any leftover pork for sandwiches.

*Note: To test for medium-low heat, you should be able to hold your hand over the heat at the height of the food for 5 seconds.

Ray's Iowa Satay

MAKES 6 SERVINGS.

Five-spice powder jazzes up marinated, skewered flank steak. This seasoning blend, often used in Chinese cooking, mixes cinnamon, cloves, fennel seeds, star anise, and Szechwan peppercorns. It's available at most large supermarkets and Asian groceries.

1	pound beef flank steak, cut across the grain into ¼-inch-thick strips
¼	cup sweet rice cooking wine
¼	cup tamari sauce or soy sauce
2	tablespoons oyster sauce (optional)
1	teaspoon chopped fresh ginger or ⅛ teaspoon ground ginger
2	cloves garlic, minced
¼	teaspoon black pepper
¼	teaspoon five-spice powder
6	10- to 12-inch wooden skewers

Prep: 10 minutes Marinate: 2 hours
Grill: 8 minutes
Nutrition facts per serving: 132 cal., 5 g fat,
31 mg chol., 376 mg sodium, 1 g carbo.,
0 g fiber, 17 g pro.

1. Place steak strips in a large self-sealing plastic bag. Add remaining ingredients to bag, tossing to coat meat. Seal bag and marinate in the refrigerator for 2 to 4 hours, turning bag occasionally. Meanwhile, soak the wooden skewers in water for 1 hour.

2. Drain meat, reserving marinade. Skewer meat accordion-style on wooden skewers. Place meat on the rack of an uncovered grill directly over medium coals. Grill, uncovered, 8 to 12 minutes or until desired doneness, turning once halfway through grilling time and brushing with marinade. Discard any remaining marinade.

When your first tomatoes turn ruby red

on the vine and your fresh herbs seem

to spill out of their pots, what better

way to show off your green thumb than

Fresh from the Garden

preparing a delectable dish featuring your

blue ribbon harvest?

Grilled Squash and More, page 56

Herb Butter

MAKES ½ CUP, 8 (1-TABLESPOON) SERVINGS.

This herbed butter makes it easy to enliven vegetables, fish, and meats or to add something special to a slice of homemade bread. For the freshest flavor, use unsalted butter and fresh lemon juice.

½ cup unsalted butter, slightly softened

¼ cup lightly packed assorted fresh herbs, such as basil, chives, oregano, savory, thyme, tarragon and Italian parsley, tough stems removed

½ teaspoon lemon juice

¼ teaspoon salt (optional)

⅛ teaspoon ground white pepper

Prep: 15 minutes Chill: 3 hours Stand: 30 minutes
Nutrition facts per tablespoon: 108 cal.,
12 g fat, 33 mg chol., 2 mg sodium,
0 g carbo., 0 g fiber, 0 g pro.

1. In a food processor bowl, combine butter, herbs, lemon juice, salt (if you like) and white pepper. Cover and process until combined.

2. Transfer mixture to a small bowl. Cover and refrigerate for at least 3 hours before serving. Store, covered, in the refrigerator for up to 2 weeks. (Or shape the chilled butter mixture into a 6-inch log. Wrap log in freezer wrap and freeze for up to 3 months. Before serving, thaw in the refrigerator for several hours or overnight.)

3. To serve, let stand at room temperature for 30 minutes. Serve on warm bread, baked potatoes, cooked vegetables or with grilled chicken, fish, chops or steaks.

Choose-an-Herb Jelly

MAKES 5 HALF-PINTS.

Savor your fresh herbs all year long in jelly. Start with your favorite herb for the first batch, then try others. "The one I like is pineapple sage," says Rosemary Divock, owner of Rosemary's Country Garden in Lake Geneva, Wisconsin. "It makes great jelly."

2 to 3 ounces freshly picked herb sprigs and/or edible flower petals *, such as, nasturtiums, pansies, violets and violas, rose petals, calendulas, marigolds, dianthuses, daylilies and/or geraniums (1 or more types of herbs or petals according to taste)
3 cups unsweetened apple juice
¼ cup lemon juice
1 1¾-ounce package regular powdered fruit pectin
Few drops yellow food coloring (optional)
4 cups sugar

Prep: 45 minutes Cook: 6 minutes
Stand: 10 minutes Process: 5 minutes
Nutrition facts per tablespoon: 44 cal., 0 g fat, 0 mg chol., 2 mg sodium, 11 g carbo., 0 g fiber, 0 g pro.

1. Gently wash herb sprigs and/or flower petals in water. Drain; place on paper towels and gently blot. Chop herbs with stems attached. Press leaves and stems or flower petals firmly into measuring cups to make 1 to 1½ cups; transfer to an 8- or 10-quart Dutch oven or kettle. Add apple juice.

2. Bring to boiling over high heat. Boil, uncovered, for 5 minutes. Remove from heat. Cover and let stand for 10 minutes.

3. Line a strainer or colander with a double layer of 100-percent-cotton cheesecloth. Strain herb and/or flower mixture through cheesecloth, pressing to extract all juice. Measure juice mixture; if necessary, add enough apple juice to equal 3 cups. Discard herb and/or flower mixture.

4. In the same Dutch oven, combine the apple juice mixture, lemon juice, fruit pectin and food coloring, if you like. Heat on high, stirring constantly until mixture comes to a full rolling boil. Add sugar all at once. Return to boiling; boil for 1 minute, stirring constantly. Remove from heat; quickly skim off foam with a metal spoon.

5. Immediately ladle jelly into hot, sterilized half-pint canning jars, leaving ¼-inch headspace. Wipe jar rims and adjust lids. Process jars in a boiling-water canner for 5 minutes (start timing when water begins to boil). Remove jars from canner; cool on racks.

*Note: The best edible flowers are unsprayed blossoms from your own garden. You also can find edible flowers in the produce section of some supermarkets, local herb gardens, mail-order outlets and some restaurant or produce suppliers. Use flowers that have been grown without the use of pesticides or other chemicals. Don't use flowers from florist shops—they're usually treated with chemicals.

Egg and Cress
Tea Sandwiches

MAKES 6 SERVINGS.

Linda Finger, who owns a guest cottage in South Yorkshire, England, includes this easy British teatime classic in the menu for a garden party she hosts in her full-time home located in Grosse Pointe Park, Michigan.

2 hard-cooked eggs, peeled and finely chopped

2 tablespoons snipped fresh watercress, chives or parsley

1 tablespoon mayonnaise or salad dressing

⅛ teaspoon salt

⅛ teaspoon ground white pepper

1 tablespoon chopped olives (optional)

4 thin slices home-style whole wheat and/or white bread

1 tablespoon butter, softened
Olive pieces (optional)

Start to Finish: 25 minutes
Nutrition facts per serving: 97 cal., 6 g fat, 77 mg chol., 178 mg sodium, 7 g carbo., 1 g fiber, 3 g pro.

1. In a small bowl, stir together the eggs, watercress, mayonnaise, salt and pepper with a fork until combined. Stir in olives, if you like.

2. Trim crusts from bread. Butter 1 side of each slice. Spread the egg mixture on 2 of the buttered bread slices. Top with remaining bread slices, buttered side down. Press lightly together.

3. Cut each of the 2 sandwiches into 3 fingers. Secure with toothpicks decorated with olive pieces, if you like. Arrange on a serving platter.

Beef-on-Rye Canapés

Herbs fresh from the garden added to cream cheese and chopped roast beef make a tasty twist on traditional English appetizers. The next time you're up for tea in the garden or simply craving a light lunch, these little bites are just right. See photo, page 37.

4 ounces deli-style roast beef, finely chopped

½ of an 8-ounce tub cream cheese

2 tablespoons finely chopped green onion

⅛ teaspoon freshly ground black pepper

⅛ teaspoon ground mace

24 slices party rye or white bread *
Fresh herbs, such as chives, oregano or basil and/or sliced radishes, cucumber, green onion tops or olives (optional)

Prep: 25 minutes Chill: up to 24 hours
Nutrition facts per canapé: 48 cal., 2 g fat, 6 mg chol., 111 mg sodium, 5 g carbo., 1 g fiber, 2 g pro.

1. In a medium bowl, combine roast beef, cream cheese, green onion, black pepper and mace. Cover and chill up to 24 hours.

2. To assemble the canapés, spread 1 to 2 teaspoons of the beef mixture on each bread slice. If you like, garnish with fresh herbs or other toppings of your choice.

*Note: If you like, use a cookie cutter to cut white bread into rounds or other desired shapes.

Lemon-on-Lemon Carrot Soup

MAKES 8 TO 10 SIDE-DISH SERVINGS.

This delightful side-dish soup is the perfect way to showcase garden-fresh carrots. The lemon thyme and fresh lemon slices add a double dose of refreshing citrus flavor. If you don't have lemon thyme on hand, regular thyme will work as well.

5   cups chicken broth
4   cups carrots, peeled and cut into ½-inch slices
3   leeks, sliced (1 cup)
1   bay leaf
3   tablespoons fresh lemon juice
2   to 3 tablespoons snipped fresh lemon thyme or thyme, or 2 to 3 teaspoons dried thyme, crushed
1   teaspoon snipped fresh summer savory (optional)
    Freshly ground black pepper
1   lemon, thinly sliced
    Fresh lemon thyme or thyme sprigs (optional)

Prep: 30 minutes Cook: 25 minutes
Nutrition facts per serving: 69 cal., 1 g fat, 0 mg chol., 511 mg sodium, 11 g carbo., 2 g fiber, 4 g pro.

1. In a large saucepan, combine the chicken broth, carrots, leeks and bay leaf. Bring to boiling; reduce heat. Simmer, covered, for 20 minutes. Add lemon juice, snipped thyme, savory (if you like) and pepper. Simmer, covered, for 5 minutes more or until carrots are tender. Cool slightly.

2. Remove bay leaf; discard. Place one-third of the carrot mixture in a food processor bowl or blender container. Cover and process or blend until smooth. Repeat with the remaining mixture. Return all to saucepan; heat through.

3. To serve, ladle the soup into bowls. Top each serving with lemon slices and, if you like, lemon thyme or thyme sprigs.

Test Kitchen Tip: Halve this recipe to make 4 to 5 side-dish servings.

Garden Corn and Black Bean Salad

Bursting with fresh flavors of the season, this colorful salad from David Hannan, a personal trainer in Kettering, Ohio, is loaded with vitamins A and C, and packs a wallop in fiber too.

4   fresh ears of corn, husked and cleaned, or 2 cups frozen whole kernel corn, thawed
1   tablespoon olive oil
1   fresh jalapeño chile pepper, seeded and finely chopped*
1   15-ounce can black beans, rinsed and drained
1   large red sweet pepper, cut into 1-inch pieces
1   cup cherry tomatoes, halved
4   green onions, bias-sliced into ½-inch pieces (½ cup)
½   cup chopped red onion
     Cilantro-Lime Salad Dressing
     Lettuce leaves (optional)

Prep: 25 minutes Cook: 2 minutes Chill: 6 hours
Nutrition facts per serving: 134 cal., 5 g fat, 1 mg chol., 632 mg sodium, 22 g carbo., 5 g fiber, 5 g pro.

1. For salad: If using fresh corn, cut kernels from cobs (should have 2 cups). In a large skillet, heat oil over medium-high heat; add corn and jalapeño. Cook, stirring frequently, for 2 to 3 minutes or until corn is lightly browned.

2. Transfer corn mixture to a large bowl and cool slightly. Stir in black beans, sweet pepper, tomatoes, green onions and red onion.

3. Immediately pour Cilantro-Lime Salad Dressing over the corn mixture. Cover and refrigerate salad for at least 6 hours or overnight.

4. To serve, toss lightly and transfer to a salad bowl. If you like, garnish with lettuce leaves.

Cilantro-Lime Salad Dressing: In a screw-top jar combine ¾ cup reduced-calorie Italian salad dressing; 2 tablespoons snipped fresh cilantro or parsley; 2 tablespoons lime juice; ½ teaspoon bottled hot pepper sauce; 1 clove garlic, minced; ¾ teaspoon salt and ½ teaspoon ground cumin. Cover and shake well.

*Test Kitchen Tip: When seeding and chopping a fresh chile pepper, protect your hands with plastic gloves; the oils in the pepper can irritate your skin. Also, avoid direct contact with your eyes. If you touch the chile pepper, wash your hands thoroughly.

Herb-Lover's Salad

MAKES 4 TO 6 SERVINGS.

"The nice thing about making your own dressing is having some fresh-from-your-garden flavor," says Rosemary Divock of Lake Geneva, Wisconsin. She tosses edible flowers and greens with homemade vinaigrette and adds snipped fresh tarragon, marjoram and chives.

8   cups mesclun (mixed baby greens) or torn mixed greens

½   cup olive oil

⅓   cup white wine vinegar

2   teaspoons snipped fresh tarragon

2   teaspoons snipped fresh marjoram

2   teaspoons snipped fresh chives

1   to 2 cloves garlic, minced
    Salt and freshly ground black pepper

2   cups petals from freshly picked edible flowers*, such as chives (with flowers), chervil, coriander, nasturtiums, pansies, violets and violas, rose petals, calendulas, marigolds, dianthuses, daylilies and/or geraniums

Prep: 10 minutes Chill: 1 hour Stand: 20 minutes
Nutrition facts per serving: 138 cal., 14 g fat, 0 mg chol., 11 mg sodium, 3 g carbo., 2 g fiber, 1 g pro.

1. For salad greens: In a large bowl of cold water, immerse the salad greens. After a few minutes, lift out the greens. Immerse the greens again, if necessary, to remove any dirt or sand particles. Discard the water. Drain the greens in a colander.

2. Place the greens on a clean kitchen towel or several layers of paper towels; gently pat dry. (Or use a salad spinner to spin the greens dry.) Wrap dried greens in a dry kitchen towel or paper towels; refrigerate for at least 1 hour or up to several hours to crisp.

3. For vinaigrette: In a screw-top jar, combine the olive oil, vinegar, tarragon, marjoram, chives and garlic. Cover; shake well to mix. Season to taste with salt and pepper. Serve immediately. (Or cover and store any remaining vinaigrette in the refrigerator for up to 1 week. Let stand at room temperature for 20 minutes before serving; shake well.)

4. For edible flowers: Gently wash the flowers in water. Drain; place on paper towels and let air-dry or gently blot dry. Use immediately.

5. To serve, arrange the greens on a large serving platter or in a salad bowl. Arrange edible flowers on top of greens. Shake the vinaigrette well; drizzle desired amount over salad. Toss gently to coat. Serve immediately. Pass additional vinaigrette, if you like.

*Note: The best edible flowers are unsprayed blossoms from your own garden. You also can find edible flowers in the produce section of some supermarkets, local herb gardens, mail-order outlets and some restaurant or produce suppliers. Use flowers that have been grown without the use of pesticides or other chemicals. Don't use flowers from florist shops—they're usually treated with chemicals.

Rosemary Biscuits

MAKES 12 BISCUITS.

Highly aromatic, rosemary lends a lemon, almost pinelike scent. Together the whole wheat flour and rosemary give these biscuits a nutty herb flavor. It's a new twist on an old favorite. Try them with soup or salad.

1	cup whole wheat flour
1	cup unbleached all-purpose flour or all-purpose flour
1	tablespoon snipped fresh rosemary or 1 teaspoon dried rosemary, crushed
2	teaspoons sugar
2	teaspoons baking powder
1	teaspoon baking soda
¼	teaspoon salt
¼	cup unsalted butter
¾	cup milk

Prep: 20 minutes Bake: 16 minutes Oven: 400°F
Nutrition facts per biscuit: 115 cal., 5 g fat, 12 mg chol., 229 mg sodium, 16 g carbo., 2 g fiber, 3 g pro.

1. Lightly grease a baking sheet; set aside. In a medium bowl, stir together the flours, rosemary, sugar, baking powder, baking soda and salt. Using a pastry blender, cut in butter until mixture resembles coarse crumbs. Make a well in the center of the flour mixture. Add the milk all at once. Using a fork, stir the mixture until just moistened.

2. Turn the dough out onto a lightly floured surface. Quickly knead the dough by gently folding and pressing 10 to 12 strokes or until nearly smooth. Pat or lightly roll dough into an 8-inch square. Cut the dough into 12 biscuits.

3. Place biscuits close together on prepared baking sheet. Bake in a 400° oven for 16 to 18 minutes or until golden. Remove biscuits from baking sheet and serve hot. Or transfer biscuits to a wire rack; cool.

Herbed Country
Twist Bread

MAKES 1 LOAF (16 SERVINGS).

Rosemary Divock, owner of an herb shop in Lake Geneva, Wisconsin, adds a different herb to each rope of this braided bread, including her namesake, rosemary. You can combine them all and add them to the whole batch of dough, if you like.

1	package active dry yeast
1	teaspoon sugar
¼	cup warm water (110°F to 115°F)
1	cup water
1	tablespoon butter, melted
1	teaspoon salt
3¼	to 3¾ cups all-purpose flour
1	tablespoon snipped fresh oregano or 1 teaspoon dried oregano, crushed
1	tablespoon snipped fresh thyme or 1 teaspoon dried thyme, crushed
1	tablespoon snipped fresh rosemary or 1 teaspoon dried rosemary, crushed
1	tablespoon butter, melted
	Grated or finely shredded Parmesan cheese (optional)

Prep: 40 minutes Rise: 1½ hours
Bake: 25 minutes Oven: 375°F
Nutrition facts per serving: 101 cal., 2 g fat, 4 mg chol., 162 mg sodium, 18 g carbo., 1 g fiber, 3 g pro.

1. In a large bowl, dissolve the yeast and sugar in the ¼ cup warm water. Set the mixture aside for 5 to 10 minutes or until foamy. Stir in the 1 cup water, the 1 tablespoon melted butter and salt. Using a wooden spoon, beat in enough flour, ½ cup at a time, to make a slightly sticky dough.

2. Turn dough out onto a lightly floured surface. Knead in enough of the remaining flour to make a dough that's smooth and elastic (6 to 8 minutes total). Shape the dough into a ball. Place in a lightly greased bowl, turning once to grease surface of the dough. Cover and let rise in a warm place until double in size (45 to 60 minutes).

3. Punch dough down. Turn the dough onto a lightly floured surface. Divide dough into thirds. For 1 of the portions, knead in the oregano. Shape the oregano dough into a ball. Repeat with the 2 remaining portions using the thyme and rosemary. Cover the three herb-flavored balls and let rest for 10 minutes. Meanwhile, lightly grease a very large baking sheet.

4. Roll each portion into a 20-inch-long rope, tapering the ends of the ropes. To shape, place the 3 ropes 1 inch apart on the prepared baking sheet. Loosely braid the 3 ropes of dough together. Press ends together to seal; tuck them under the loaf.

5. Cover and let rise in a warm place until nearly double (about 45 minutes). Brush the loaf with the remaining 1 tablespoon melted butter and sprinkle top with Parmesan, if you like.

6. Bake in a 375° oven for 25 to 30 minutes or until bread is golden brown and sounds hollow when you tap the top with your fingers. Immediately remove bread from baking sheet. Cool on a wire rack.

Lemony Tea Bread

MAKES 1 LOAF (16 SERVINGS).

Any lemon-flavored herb will work in this sweet, cakelike quick bread. Rosemary Divock likes to bake a few loaves to slice and offer to customers at her shop in Lake Geneva, Wisconsin. It's great with coffee too!

¾ cup milk

3 tablespoons snipped fresh lemon balm, lemon thyme and/or lemon verbena

2 cups all-purpose flour

2 teaspoons baking powder

¼ teaspoon salt

½ cup butter, softened

1 cup granulated sugar

2 eggs

1 tablespoon finely shredded lemon peel

¾ cup sifted powdered sugar

3 tablespoons lemon juice
  Fresh lemon thyme sprigs (optional)

Prep: 35 minutes Bake: 50 minutes
Cool: 10 minutes Oven: 325°F
Nutrition facts per serving: 187 cal., 7 g fat, 44 mg chol., 162 mg sodium, 29 g carbo., 1 g fiber, 3 g pro.

1. In a small saucepan, combine milk and lemon balm, lemon thyme, and/or lemon verbena. Bring to just boiling; remove from heat. Let stand at room temperature for 20 minutes to cool.

2. Grease and lightly flour the bottom and ½ inch up the sides of a 9×5×3-inch loaf pan; set aside. In a medium bowl, combine the flour, baking powder and salt; set aside.

3. In a large mixing bowl, beat butter with an electric mixer for 30 seconds. Add sugar; beat until well combined. Add eggs, one at a time, beating after each addition. Add flour mixture and milk mixture alternately to butter mixture, beating on low speed after each addition until just combined. Stir in lemon peel. Pour batter into the prepared pan.

4. Bake in a 325° oven for 50 to 55 minutes or until a wooden toothpick inserted near the center comes out clean.

5. Cool loaf in the pan on a wire rack for 10 minutes. Meanwhile, whisk together the powdered sugar and lemon juice. Place a sheet of waxed paper under the wire rack. Remove loaf from pan; return to wire rack. Immediately drizzle or brush the lemon-sugar mixture over top of the hot loaf. Cool bread completely on the wire rack.

6. To serve, slice bread and arrange on a serving plate. Garnish with sprigs of lemon thyme, if you like.

Streusel-Topped Pumpkin Muffins

MAKES 12 MUFFINS.

Dried fruit, lemon peel and spices are tucked into this classic pumpkin bread batter. Sprinkled with a crunchy sugar topping, it's a muffin worth waking up for in the morning. Store any remaining muffins in your freezer for up to 3 months.

1½	cups all-purpose flour
¾	cup rolled oats
2	teaspoons baking powder
1½	teaspoons finely shredded lemon peel
1½	teaspoons ground cinnamon
¼	teaspoon baking soda
¼	teaspoon ground allspice
⅛	teaspoon salt
1	beaten egg
¾	cup milk
¾	cup canned pumpkin
½	cup packed brown sugar
¼	cup cooking oil
¾	cup chopped dried figs or chopped pitted dates
	Streusel Topping

Prep: 20 minutes Bake: 20 to 25 minutes
Cool: 5 minutes Oven: 400°F
Nutrition facts per muffin: 257 cal., 8 g fat,
24 mg chol., 159 mg sodium, 43 g carbo.,
3 g fiber, 4 g pro.

1. Lightly grease twelve 2½-inch muffin cups; set aside. In a medium bowl, combine flour, oats, baking powder, lemon peel, cinnamon, baking soda, allspice and salt. Make a well in center of flour mixture.

2. In another medium bowl, combine egg, milk, pumpkin, brown sugar and oil. Add all at once to flour mixture. Stir just until moistened (batter should be lumpy). Fold in figs.

3. Spoon batter into prepared muffin cups, filling each three-fourths full. Sprinkle batter with Streusel Topping. Bake in a 400° oven for 20 to 25 minutes or until wooden toothpicks inserted in centers come out clean. Cool in muffin cups on a wire rack for 5 minutes. Remove from muffin cups; serve warm.

Streusel Topping: Stir together ⅓ cup packed brown sugar, ¼ cup all-purpose flour and ½ teaspoon ground cinnamon. Cut in 2 tablespoons butter until mixture resembles coarse crumbs.

Garden-Special Primavera

MAKES 6 MAIN-DISH SERVINGS.

From crisp, tender green beans to zucchini, this easy pasta dish takes advantage of the garden's bounty. Tossed in a light and creamy sauce, this is a delicate, yet substantial, main dish.

6	ounces fresh wax or green beans
6	ounces fresh asparagus
½	cup bias-sliced carrot
1	cup broccoli florets
12	ounces dried fettuccine
1	small red and/or yellow sweet pepper, cut into julienne strips
1	small zucchini or yellow summer squash, halved lengthwise and sliced (1 cup)
1	small onion, cut into wedges
2	cloves garlic, minced
2	tablespoons butter
¾	cup chicken broth
¾	cup whipping cream
2	tablespoons all-purpose flour
½	cup finely shredded Parmesan cheese
2	ounces prosciutto or cooked ham, cut into thin strips (⅓ cup)
2	green onions, thinly sliced (¼ cup)
2	tablespoons snipped fresh basil

Start to Finish: 45 minutes
Nutrition facts per serving: 457 cal., 20 g fat, 67 mg chol., 549 mg sodium, 53 g carbo., 4 g fiber, 16 g pro.

1. Cut fresh beans into 2-inch pieces (should have 2 cups). Trim asparagus and cut into 2-inch pieces (should have 1½ cups); set aside. In a large saucepan, cook beans and carrots in a small amount of boiling salted water for 10 minutes. Add asparagus and broccoli. Return to boiling; reduce heat. Cover and cook 5 minutes more or until vegetables are crisp-tender. Drain.

2. Meanwhile, in a large saucepan, cook pasta according to package directions. Add sweet pepper and zucchini to pasta in boiling water for the last 3 minutes of cooking. Vegetables should be crisp-tender. Drain and return pasta mixture to the saucepan. Add the bean mixture to the saucepan; keep warm while preparing sauce.

3. For sauce: In a medium saucepan, cook onion and garlic in hot butter over medium heat for 5 to 8 minutes or until tender, but not brown. Stir in chicken broth. Bring to boiling; reduce heat.

4. In a small bowl, stir together whipping cream and flour. Add cream mixture to saucepan. Cook and stir until thickened and bubbly. Stir in the Parmesan cheese, prosciutto, green onions and basil. Cook and stir for 1 minute more. Pour sauce over pasta and vegetables. Toss gently to coat.

5. Arrange pasta mixture on a large serving platter. Sprinkle with additional Parmesan, if you like.

Nine-Herb Pasta

If you only have a couple of these herbs on hand, try the recipe using what you have. Just don't skip the garlic, crushed red pepper, salt or pepper. To indulge, top with freshly shredded Parmesan cheese.

1	pound tripolini (tiny bow ties), ditalini (thimbles) or ruote (wagon wheels) pasta
1/3	to 1/2 cup olive oil
1	tablespoon snipped fresh Italian parsley
1	tablespoon snipped fresh basil
2	teaspoons snipped fresh chives
2	teaspoons snipped fresh chervil
1	teaspoon snipped fresh tarragon
1	teaspoon snipped fresh sage
1	teaspoon snipped fresh oregano
1	teaspoon snipped fresh marjoram
1	teaspoon snipped fresh rosemary
2	cloves garlic, minced
1/2	teaspoon crushed red pepper
	Finely shredded Parmesan cheese (optional)

Start to Finish: 35 minutes
Nutrition facts per serving: 291 cal., 10 g fat, 0 mg chol., 39 mg sodium, 43 g carbo., 1 g fiber, 7 g pro.

1. Cook tripolini pasta according to package directions. Drain; transfer pasta to a large bowl. Cover and keep warm.

2. In a medium skillet, heat the olive oil over medium heat. Add the herbs, garlic and crushed red pepper. Cook and gently stir for 2 to 3 minutes or until herbs turn bright green, releasing their fragrance.

3. Stir the herb mixture into pasta. Season to taste with salt and freshly ground black pepper. Sprinkle with Parmesan, if you like. Serve immediately.

Herbed Gruyère Ring

MAKES 5 SERVINGS.

This delicious brunch dish fills a simple cream puff ring with a colorful mixture of assorted stir-fried vegetables, herbs and chicken. The Gruyère Ring is also a great way to dress up your favorite tuna or egg salad recipe.

Gruyère Ring
- 2 tablespoons butter, softened
- 1 tablespoon snipped fresh Italian parsley or regular parsley
- 1 teaspoon snipped fresh chives
- 2 tablespoons butter
- 1 cup sliced carrots
- 1 cup cauliflower florets
- 1 medium zucchini and/or yellow summer squash, halved lengthwise and cut into ½-inch slices
- 1 cup snow peas, cut crosswise in half; asparagus spears, cut into 2-inch pieces, or 2-inch green onion pieces
- 12 ounces skinless, boneless chicken breast halves, cut into 1-inch cubes
- 1 tablespoon snipped fresh basil Sprigs of fresh basil, Italian parsley and chives (optional)

Prep: 45 minutes Bake: 40 minutes
Cool: 1 hour 10 minutes Oven: 400°F
Nutrition facts per serving: 410 cal., 26 g fat, 189 mg chol., 547 mg sodium, 19 g carbo., 2 g fiber, 25 g pro.

1. Prepare Gruyère Ring. When Gruyère Ring is cool, use a serrated knife to cut ring in half horizontally. Remove and discard the weblike centers, if you like.

2. In a small bowl, combine the 2 tablespoons softened butter, the snipped Italian parsley, snipped chives, ¼ teaspoon salt and pepper. Set aside.

3. In a 12-inch skillet, heat remaining 2 tablespoons butter over medium heat. (Add additional butter, if needed, during cooking.) Add carrots and cauliflower; stir-fry for 3 minutes. Add remaining vegetables and stir-fry 3 to 4 minutes or until all vegetables are crisp-tender.

4. Remove vegetables from skillet. Add chicken and snipped basil to the skillet and stir-fry 3 to 4 minutes or until chicken is no longer pink. Return all vegetables to skillet; add butter mixture and toss to coat.

5. To serve, place bottom half of Gruyère Ring on a serving plate. Spoon the chicken mixture over bottom half of Gruyère Ring. Replace the top of the ring. Spoon any remaining chicken and vegetable mixture in center of the ring. Garnish with sprigs of basil, Italian parsley and whole chives, if you like. Serve immediately.

Gruyère Ring: In a medium saucepan, combine ⅔ cup water, ¼ cup butter and ¼ teaspoon salt. Bring to boiling. Add ⅔ cup all-purpose flour all at once, stirring vigorously. Cook and stir until mixture forms a ball. Remove from heat. Cool for 10 minutes. Add 2 eggs, one at a time, beating well with a wooden spoon after each addition. Stir in all but 1 tablespoon of ½ cup finely shredded natural Gruyère or Swiss cheese (2 ounces). Drop dough by large spoonfuls, forming 10 mounds, in a 10-inch ring on a greased 12-inch pizza pan. Sprinkle remaining 1 tablespoon of cheese over top of dough. Bake in a 400° oven for 40 minutes or until puffed and golden. Cool on pan on a wire rack.

Gingered Autumn Chutney

MAKES 10 (¼-CUP) SERVINGS.

This fruity, chunky condiment balances the sweet and spicy with a kick of vinegar just for fun. It's a perfect accompaniment for roasted or grilled meat that so often graces a Sunday menu.

¾	cup chopped red onion
⅔	cup sugar
⅔	cup red wine vinegar
⅓	cup golden raisins
2	teaspoons grated fresh ginger
2	teaspoons finely shredded lemon peel
1	teaspoon mustard seeds
½	teaspoon ground cumin
¼	teaspoon ground red pepper
2½	cups seeded and chopped tomatoes (about 5 medium)
2½	cups chopped, cored and peeled pears (2 large)

Prep: 15 minutes Cook: 45 minutes
Nutrition facts per ¼-cup serving: 106 cal.,
0 g fat, 0 mg chol., 6 mg sodium,
26 g carbo., 2 g fiber, 1 g pro.

1. In a large saucepan, combine the onion, sugar, vinegar, raisins, ginger, lemon peel, mustard seeds, cumin and red pepper. Bring to boiling; reduce heat. Simmer, covered, for 10 minutes.

2. Stir tomatoes and pears into onion mixture. Return to boiling; reduce heat. Simmer, uncovered, for 35 minutes or until chutney is thickened, stirring frequently. Serve chutney warm or chilled with ham, turkey or pork.

3. Cover and chill leftover chutney for up to 3 days or freeze for up to 3 months. Reheat in saucepan or serve cold (thaw frozen chutney overnight in refrigerator).

Orange-Glazed Sweet Potatoes

MAKES 6 SERVINGS.

Brown sugar, butter and orange—a trio of ingredients perfectly made to enrobe sweet potatoes. Who would know better than the family that grows the potatoes, the Tiemeyers of Vallonia, Indiana. It's their recipe.

2	pounds sweet potatoes
2	tablespoons butter or margarine
⅓	cup packed brown sugar or granulated sugar
1	tablespoon cornstarch
½	teaspoon salt
¼	teaspoon ground nutmeg (optional)
½	teaspoon finely shredded orange peel
¾	cup orange juice

Prep: 25 minutes Bake: 40 minutes Oven: 400°F
Nutrition facts per serving: 215 cal.,
4 g fat, 11 mg chol., 254 mg sodium,
43 g carbo., 3 g fiber, 2 g pro.

1. Peel the potatoes; halve lengthwise. Arrange pieces in a 13×9×2-inch greased baking dish (3-quart rectangular).

2. For sauce: In a medium saucepan, melt butter. Stir in brown sugar, cornstarch, salt and nutmeg, if you like. Stir in orange peel and juice. Cook and stir over medium heat until thickened and bubbly.

3. Pour sauce over the sweet potato pieces. Bake, covered, in a 400° oven for 40 to 45 minutes or until potatoes are tender, spooning liquid over potatoes once. To serve, spoon sauce over potatoes.

Parslied New Potatoes

MAKES 6 SERVINGS.

New potatoes fresh from the earth—there's nothing as basic nor as delicious. Patty Tiemeyer blends their crop of parsley with these tubers, cooked in chicken broth and onion. It's the perfect accompaniment for any meat or poultry dish.

15	to 18 tiny new potatoes (about 1½ pounds)
1	tablespoon olive oil
1	medium onion, chopped (½ cup)
1	clove garlic, minced
1	cup chicken broth
⅔	cup snipped fresh parsley
½	teaspoon freshly ground black pepper
	Salt

Prep: 20 minutes Cook: 12 minutes
Nutrition facts per serving: 117 cal., 3 g fat, 0 mg chol., 179 mg sodium, 21 g carbo., 2 g fiber, 3 g pro.

1. To wash potatoes, lightly scrub the skins under running water. Cut any large potatoes in half. If you like, remove a narrow strip of peel from around the center of each whole potato; set aside.

2. In a 12-inch skillet, heat the oil over medium heat. Add onion and garlic. Cook and stir over medium heat until onion is tender. Add the chicken broth, ⅓ cup of the parsley and black pepper. Carefully arrange the potatoes in a single layer in the broth mixture. Bring to boiling; reduce heat. Simmer, covered, for 12 to 15 minutes or just until tender. Season to taste with salt.

3. To serve, transfer potatoes and broth mixture to a large serving bowl. Sprinkle with the remaining ⅓ cup parsley.

Grilled Squash and More

MAKES 4 TO 6 SERVINGS.

Italian dressing leaves an herbed vinegar glaze on the onion, mushrooms and squash. Cook the veggies on your outdoor grill or use an indoor electric grill. Either way it cooks fast, just the way Patty Tiemeyer cooks after a long day at her family's roadside market.

3   medium zucchini and/or yellow summer squash, cut lengthwise into quarters

1   medium red onion, cut cross-wise into ½-inch-thick slices

8   ounces fresh mushrooms, stems removed

½   cup bottled Italian salad dressing*

Fresh rosemary sprigs (optional)

Prep: 15 minutes Grill: 8 minutes/Broil: 12 minutes
Nutrition facts per serving: 179 cal., 15 g fat, 0 mg chol., 239 mg sodium, 10 g carbo., 2 g fiber, 4 g pro.

1. To grill: Brush zucchini and/or squash, onion slices and mushrooms with some of the salad dressing. Grill the vegetables (if using indoor electric grill, you may have to grill vegetables half at a time) on the rack of an uncovered grill directly over medium to medium-hot coals or heat source (for indoor electric grill) about 8 minutes or until crisp-tender and lightly brown, turning and brushing once with remaining salad dressing. Arrange on a platter to serve. Garnish wih rosemary sprigs, if you like.

2. To broil: Place zucchini and/or squash, onion slices and mushrooms on the unheated rack of a broiler pan. Brush the vegetables with some of the salad dressing. Broil 3 inches from heat for 12 minutes or until crisp-tender and lightly brown, turning and brushing once with remaining salad dressing.

*Note: For a zestier dressing, stir ½ teaspoon finely shredded lemon peel, 2 tablespoons lemon juice, 1 tablespoon Dijon-style mustard and ¼ teaspoon crushed red pepper into Italian salad dressing before brushing on veggies.

Fruit Bowl with a Punch

MAKES 6 SERVINGS.

Adding hot chile peppers to a sugar syrup for fruit may sound strange, but the end product will surprise you. The sweet, fiery finish to melons and fall fruit is so simple, yet so tantalizing. Not up for the excitement? Make it without the peppers.

¾ cup water

½ cup sugar

1 to 2 fresh serrano chile peppers*, halved lengthwise

2 teaspoons finely shredded lime peel

4 teaspoons lime juice

3 cups melon balls (watermelon, cantaloupe and/or honeydew)

1 large apple or pear, cored and cut into chunks

2 medium plums, pitted and sliced

Prep: 10 minutes Cool: 45 minutes Chill: 1 hour
Nutrition facts per serving: 119 cal., 1 g fat, 0 mg chol., 3 mg sodium, 30 g carbo., 2 g fiber, 1 g pro.

1. For syrup: In a small saucepan, combine water, sugar, serrano peppers and lime juice. Bring to boiling; reduce heat. Simmer, uncovered, for 3 minutes. Remove from heat; cool to room temperature.

2. Strain syrup into a large serving bowl; discard peppers and seeds. Stir in lime peel. Add melon balls, apple and plums; stir gently to coat. Cover and chill for 1 to 4 hours before serving.

Note: For a milder flavor, serrano chile peppers may be omitted.

Champagne and Brandied Fruit

MAKES 12 (4-OUNCE) SERVINGS.

It's a drink! It's a dessert! Linda Finger and Paula Morris, backyard neighbors from Grosse Point, Michigan, serve colorful seasonal fruit laced with a bit of bubbly in Champagne glasses. Put this on the menu the next time you want to toast a special occasion.

2   cups fresh or frozen unsweetened whole strawberries

2   cups fresh or frozen unsweetened peeled peach slices

2   cups fresh pineapple chunks
     Sugar (optional)

¼   cup brandy, rum, unsweetened pineapple juice or orange juice

1   750-milliliter bottle brut Champagne, sparkling wine, sparkling apple cider, sparkling white grape juice or 4 cups unsweetened pineapple juice, chilled

Prep: 25 minutes Chill: 6 hours
Nutrition facts per serving: 89 cal., 0 g fat, 0 mg chol., 1 mg sodium, 10 g carbo., 1 g fiber, 1 g pro.

1. In a large bowl, combine whole strawberries, peach slices and pineapple chunks. Sweeten fruit with a little sugar, if you like. Add brandy. Cover and refrigerate the mixture for 6 to 8 hours.

2. Fill wide-mouth champagne or other saucer-shaped glasses half full with fruit mixture. Just before serving, pour chilled Champagne over the fruit and fill almost to the top. Stir gently.

Fruit and Herb Crepes

MAKES 6 SERVINGS.

Sage, basil or mint adds a new flavor dimension to delicate crepes. Fill them with a yogurt-fruit mixture that brings a taste of summer to the table. Use whatever fruit combination you prefer.

3	beaten eggs
1½	cups unbleached all-purpose flour or all-purpose flour
1½	cups milk
⅓	cup unsalted butter, melted
¼	cup snipped fresh sage, basil or mint
¼	teaspoon salt
¼	teaspoon ground white pepper
1	cup sliced strawberries
1	medium banana, sliced
½	cup peeled and sliced kiwi fruit
1	cup granola
1	cup vanilla low-fat yogurt
¼	teaspoon ground cinnamon

Prep: 15 minutes Chill: 15 minutes
Cook: 4 minutes/batch
Nutrition facts per serving: 453 cal., 20 g fat, 142 mg chol., 193 mg sodium, 56 g carbo., 4 g fiber, 13 g pro.

1. For crepes: In a large mixing bowl, combine eggs, flour, milk, melted butter, sage, salt and white pepper. Beat with a wire whisk until well mixed. Cover and refrigerate for 15 to 30 minutes.

2. For fruit filling: In a medium bowl, combine the strawberries, banana and kiwi fruit. Gently stir in the granola, yogurt and cinnamon. Cover and chill while cooking the crepes.

3. Heat a lightly greased 10-inch crepe pan or nonstick skillet with flared sides over medium heat. Remove from heat. Ladle in ½ cup batter. Lift and tilt pan to spread the batter. Return to heat and cook until the bottom of crepe is light brown. Flip crepe over with a smooth motion. Continue cooking about 2 minutes or until second side is light brown. Invert pan over paper towels to remove crepe. Repeat with remaining batter, greasing pan occasionally.

4. To assemble, spoon about ½ cup of the fruit filling along the center of one side of crepe. Fold the two opposite edges so they overlap over filling. Serve immediately.

Test Kitchen Tip: For a thinner crepe, use less batter. Use regular butter and omit the salt, if you like.

Carrot-Zucchini Bars

MAKES 36 BARS.

Take your zucchini surplus and make it into a dessert. Adding both carrots and zukes doubles the fun, and cranberries give a tangy edge to the flavor. Traditional cream cheese frosting-lovers will appreciate a delicate hint of citrus from a little orange peel and juice.

2	cups all-purpose flour
2	teaspoons baking powder
2	teaspoons finely shredded orange peel
½	teaspoon baking soda
⅛	teaspoon salt
3	beaten eggs
1½	cups packed brown sugar
⅔	cup cooking oil
¼	cup milk
1½	teaspoons vanilla
1	cup finely shredded carrots
1	cup finely shredded, unpeeled zucchini
¾	cup coarsely chopped fresh or frozen cranberries
2	tablespoons finely chopped crystallized ginger (optional)
	Orange-Cream Cheese Frosting

Prep: 25 minutes Bake: 20 minutes Oven: 350°F
Nutrition facts per bar: 163 cal., 8 g fat, 26 mg chol., 86 mg sodium, 23 g carbo., 0 g fiber, 2 g pro.

1. Grease a 15×10×1-inch baking pan; set aside. In a large bowl, stir together flour, baking powder, orange peel, baking soda and salt. Set aside.

2. In a medium bowl, combine eggs, brown sugar, oil, milk and vanilla. Stir in carrots, zucchini, cranberries and ginger, if you like. Add egg mixture to flour mixture, stirring until combined. Spread batter in prepared pan.

3. Bake in a 350° oven for 20 to 25 minutes or until a wooden toothpick inserted near center comes out clean. Cool in pan on a wire rack. Spread with Orange-Cream Cheese Frosting and cut into bars. Store, covered, in the refrigerator.

Orange-Cream Cheese Frosting: In a medium mixing bowl, beat together ½ of an 8-ounce package cream cheese, softened; ⅓ cup butter, softened; 1 teaspoon finely shredded orange peel; 4 teaspoons orange juice and 1 teaspoon vanilla until combined. Gradually beat in enough sifted powdered sugar (2¾ to 3¼ cups) until frosting reaches spreading consistency.

Pumpkin Chiffon Pie

Makes 8 servings.

Try this recipe when it's time to bake that traditional pumpkin pie. Although regular pumpkin is hard to beat, this version will get your attention after the first forkful of filling— a spiced concoction developed by Patty Tiemeyer of Indiana—nestled in a gingersnap crust.

Gingersnap Crust
½ cup sugar
2 envelopes unflavored gelatin
½ teaspoon ground cinnamon
½ teaspoon ground allspice
¼ teaspoon salt
¼ teaspoon ground ginger
¼ teaspoon ground nutmeg
¾ cup milk
2 egg yolks
1 cup canned pumpkin
1 cup whipping cream
2 tablespoons sugar
   Whipped cream (optional)
   Ground cinnamon (optional)

Prep: 20 minutes Chill: 5½ hours
Nutrition facts per serving with gingersnap crust: 349 cal., 23 g fat, 118 mg chol., 299 mg sodium, 33 g carbo., 1 g fiber, 5 g pro.

1. Prepare Gingersnap Crust; set aside.

2. For filling: In a heavy medium saucepan, stir together the ½ cup sugar, gelatin, cinnamon, allspice, salt, ginger and nutmeg; stir in milk. Cook and stir over medium heat until gelatin dissolves.

3. In a medium mixing bowl, slightly beat egg yolks with a rotary beater or fork. Gradually stir about half of the hot milk mixture into yolks. Pour yolk mixture into hot filling in pan. Stir in pumpkin. Bring to a gentle boil; reduce heat. Cook and stir for 2 minutes more. Remove from heat. Transfer to a large bowl. Cover and chill until the pumpkin mixture mounds when spooned, stirring occasionally (1 to 1½ hours).

4. In a chilled medium mixing bowl, combine the whipping cream and the remaining 2 tablespoons sugar. Beat with chilled beaters of an electric mixer on medium speed until soft peaks form. Fold whipped cream into pumpkin mixture. Cover and chill again until mixture mounds when spooned (about 30 minutes).

5. Transfer filling to Gingersnap Crust. Cover and chill about 4 hours or until set (or cover and chill overnight). If you like, garnish with additional whipped cream and sprinkle lightly with ground cinnamon.

Gingersnap Crust: Combine ⅓ cup melted butter and 1¼ cups finely crushed gingersnaps (20 to 22 cookies) in a medium bowl; toss to mix well. Spread evenly into a 9-inch pie plate. Press onto bottom and up sides to form a firm, even crust. Chill about 1 hour or until firm. (Or bake in a 375° oven for 4 to 5 minutes or until edge is lightly browned. Cool on a wire rack before filling.) Makes 1 (9-inch) piecrust.

Butternut Squash in a Pie

MAKES 8 SERVINGS.

In this recipe, chubby butternut squash gets the royal treatment—it's packed into a pie. Similar to pumpkin, it's baked and mashed to fold into the filling. Spices, brown sugar and sorghum flavor this pumpkinlike pie that has a grainier texture than pumpkin.

Pastry for Single-Crust Pie

1¾	cup cooked and cooled butternut squash*
⅔	cup packed brown sugar or granulated sugar
2	tablespoons sorghum or dark molasses
1	teaspoon ground cinnamon
½	teaspoon ground ginger
¼	teaspoon ground nutmeg
¼	teaspoon ground cloves
2	eggs
1	12-ounce can evaporated milk (1½ cups)
	Whipped cream (optional)

Prep: 35 minutes Bake: 50 minutes Oven: 375°F
Nutrition facts per serving: 332 cal., 13 g fat, 67 mg chol., 148 mg sodium, 47 g carbo., 1 g fiber, 7 g pro.

1. Prepare Pastry for Single-Crust Pie. On a lightly floured surface, use your hands to slightly flatten dough ball. Roll dough from center to edge into a 12-inch circle. Wrap pastry circle around a rolling pin; unroll into a 9-inch pie plate, being careful not to stretch pastry. Trim pastry ½ inch beyond edge of pie plate. Fold under extra pastry. Crimp edge. Do not prick pastry.

2. For filling: In a large mixing bowl, combine squash, brown sugar, sorghum, cinnamon, ginger, nutmeg and cloves. Add eggs. Beat lightly with a rotary beater or fork just until combined. Gradually stir in evaporated milk; mix well. Place the pastry-lined pie plate on the oven rack. Carefully pour the filling into pastry shell.

3. To prevent overbrowning, cover edge of pie with a metal piecrust shield or foil. Bake in a 375° oven for 25 minutes. Remove shield or foil. Bake for 25 minutes more or until a knife inserted near center comes out clean. Cool on a wire rack. Refrigerate within 2 hours; cover for longer storage. If you like, serve with whipped cream.

Pastry for Single-Crust Pie: In a large bowl, stir together 1¼ cups all-purpose flour and ¼ teaspoon salt. Using a pastry blender, cut in ⅓ cup shortening until pieces are pea-size. Sprinkle 1 tablespoon of cold water over part of the mixture; gently toss with a fork. Push moistened dough to side of bowl. Repeat, using 1 tablespoon cold water at a time (4 to 5 tablespoons total), until all of the dough is moistened. Shape dough into a ball.

*Note: Wash 1 medium butternut squash (about 1¾ pounds). Halve squash lengthwise and remove seeds; discard seeds. Place the squash halves, cut sides down, in a 2-quart rectangular (12×7-inch) baking dish. Bake, uncovered, in a 350° oven for 30 minutes. Turn cut sides up. Bake, covered, 20 to 25 minutes more or until tender. Cool until easy to handle. Scoop out pulp; measure 1¾ cups.

Scented Geranium Cake

MAKES 12 SERVINGS.

The flowers from scented geraniums lend color to this delicate pound cake, and their fragrant leaves add flavor to the sugar sprinkled over the top. Be sure to stop and smell the scented geraniums. The aroma is wonderful.

24	freshly-picked scented geranium blossoms (such as rose, lemon, mint, apple or nutmeg) or 1 cup rose petals
2½	cups unbleached all-purpose flour or all-purpose flour
1	tablespoon finely shredded lemon peel
½	teaspoon salt
6	eggs
4	egg yolks
2	cups granulated sugar
1	cup unsalted butter, melted
	Rose Geranium Flavored Sugar (optional)
	Whipped cream (optional)

Prep: 25 minutes Bake: 30 minutes
Cool: 1¼ hours Oven: 375°F
Nutrition facts per serving: 412 cal.,
21 g fat, 221 mg chol., 134 mg sodium,
51 g carbo., 1 g fiber, 7 g pro.

1. Generously butter and lightly flour a 13×9×2-inch baking pan. Arrange the geranium flowers or rose petals in a single layer on bottom of prepared pan; set aside. In a medium bowl, combine flour, lemon peel and salt; set aside.

2. In a very large mixing bowl, beat eggs, egg yolks and granulated sugar with an electric mixer on medium to high speed about 6 minutes or until very thick and pale yellow, scraping bowl frequently.

3. Gently fold one-third of the flour mixture into the egg mixture. Repeat with remaining flour mixture. Gradually pour one-third of the melted butter over batter, gently folding to combine. Repeat with the remaining butter.

4. Carefully pour batter over the flowers in prepared pan. Bake in a 375° oven about 30 minutes or until a wooden toothpick inserted into the cake comes out clean and the top is light golden brown. Cool cake in the pan on a wire rack for 15 minutes. Loosen sides of cake from the pan by running a knife around edge of cake. Invert cake onto a large serving platter and cool completely.

5. To serve, sprinkle top of cake with Rose Geranium Flavored Sugar, if you like. Garnish with bouquet of fresh geranium flowers, if you like. Serve with whipped cream, if you like.

Rose Geranium Flavored Sugar: Gently wash 24 small rose-scented geranium leaves (or lemon-, mint-, apple- or nutmeg-scented leaves) or 1 cup rose petals in water. Drain; place on paper towels. Let stand, uncovered, to dry completely. In a clean 1-quart glass jar or bottle, layer geranium leaves or rose petals with 1 cup sugar or extra-fine granulated sugar. Cover jar or bottle tightly with a lid. Let stand at room temperature for at least 24 hours or for up to 1 week to absorb oils from geranium leaves or rose petals. To use, sprinkle the flavored sugar over cakes, cookies, fresh fruit, baked custard or sorbet. Makes about 1 cup.

You could travel miles to find this collection of

specialties from country inns and restaurants

scattered across the Midwest. From melt-in-

your-mouth cinnamon rolls

The Season's Best from

Country Inns and

Restaurants

to incredible beef tenderloin, these recipes

will tantalize your taste buds—all in the

comfort of your own home.

Snow-Season Pancakes, page 74

Jumbo Coffee Cake Muffins

MAKES 6 JUMBO MUFFINS.

Muffins are a specialty of baker Ali Patten at the Inn at Pinewood, 5 miles east of Eagle River, Wisconsin. These tender cinnamon-sugar delights fuel guests before they hit the trails for snowmobiling or cross-country skiing.

Nonstick cooking spray
1½	cups all-purpose flour
2	teaspoons baking powder
¼	teaspoon baking soda
¼	teaspoon salt
¼	cup shortening
1	8-ounce carton dairy sour cream or plain yogurt
½	cup granulated sugar
½	cup milk
1	beaten egg
¼	cup packed brown sugar
¼	cup chopped nuts
2	tablespoons granulated sugar
1	teaspoon ground cinnamon

Prep: 20 minutes Bake: 25 minutes
Cool: 15 minutes Oven: 350°F
Nutrition facts per muffin: 436 cal.,
21 g fat, 54 mg chol., 328 mg sodium,
56 g carbo., 1 g fiber, 7 g pro.

1. Lightly coat 6 jumbo* (3½-inch) muffin cups with cooking spray or line with paper bake cups. Set aside.

2. In a large bowl, stir together the flour, baking powder, baking soda and salt. Cut in the shortening until the mixture is crumbly.

3. In medium bowl, stir together the sour cream, the ½ cup granulated sugar, the milk and egg. Add sour cream mixture to flour mixture and stir until the mixture is just combined.

4. In a small bowl, stir together brown sugar, nuts, the 2 tablespoons granulated sugar and cinnamon.

5. Spoon half the batter into prepared muffin cups. Sprinkle half of the nut mixture into cups. Top with remaining batter and the remaining nut mixture.

6. Bake in a 350° oven about 25 minutes or until wooden toothpicks inserted in centers come out clean. Cool 15 minutes in pan on wire rack. Remove from pan and serve warm.

Note: For standard-size muffins, use 12 regular (2½-inch) muffin cups; divide batter evenly as above. Bake in 400° oven for 15 to 18 minutes. Cool 5 minutes. Remove from pans and serve warm.

North Woods
Wake-Up Muffins

MAKES 24 REGULAR OR 12 JUMBO MUFFINS.

While she bakes goodies in her kitchen at Pincushion Mountain B&B in Grand Marais, Minnesota, Mary Beattie can watch the snow fly and guests snowshoe. These amazing muffins are loaded with pecans, cream cheese, bananas, coffee and chocolate.

1	cup chopped pecans
3	tablespoons sugar
2	teaspoons ground cinnamon
1	8-ounce package cream cheese, softened
½	cup butter, softened
1¼	cups sugar
2	eggs
1	cup mashed ripe bananas (3 medium)
1	tablespoon instant coffee powder or espresso coffee powder
1	teaspoon vanilla
2¼	cups all-purpose flour
1½	teaspoons baking powder
½	teaspoon baking soda
1	cup semisweet chocolate pieces (6 ounces)

Prep: 25 minutes Bake: 20 minutes
Oven: 375°F
Nutrition facts per regular muffin: 243 cal., 13 g fat, 39 mg chol., 127 mg sodium, 30 g carbo., 2 g fiber, 3 g pro.

1. Line 24 regular (2½-inch) muffin cups or 12 jumbo (3½-inch) muffin cups with paper bake cups. In a small bowl, combine the pecans, the 3 tablespoons sugar and cinnamon; set aside.

2. In a large mixing bowl, beat together the cream cheese, butter and 1¼ cups sugar with an electric mixer until well combined.

3. Add eggs, one at a time, beating well after each addition. Beat in the bananas, coffee powder and vanilla.

4. In a medium bowl, combine the flour, baking powder and baking soda. Gradually beat the flour mixture into the cream cheese mixture on low speed until combined. Stir in the chocolate pieces.

5. Stir half of the pecan mixture into the batter. Spoon batter into muffin cups, filling about two-thirds full. Sprinkle with remaining pecan mixture.

6. Bake in a 375° oven for 20 to 22 minutes for the regular muffins and 22 to 25 minutes for the jumbo muffins or until wooden toothpicks inserted into centers come out clean. Cool 15 minutes in pan on a wire rack. Remove muffins from pan and serve warm.

Dreamy Cinnamon Breakfast Rolls

MAKES 32 ROLLS.

At the Pincushion Mountain B&B near Grand Marais, Minnesota, guests wake up anticipating Mary Beattie's baking. Her melt-in-your-mouth cinnamon rolls always bring smiles to her breakfast guests.

1	package 2-layer size French vanilla cake mix
5½	to 6 cups all-purpose flour
2	packages active dry yeast
1	teaspoon salt
2½	cups warm water (120°F to 130°F)
¼	cup butter, softened
¾	cup granulated sugar
1	tablespoon ground cinnamon
1⅓	cups packed brown sugar
1	cup butter
2	tablespoons light-colored corn syrup
1½	cups chopped walnuts

Prep: 30 minutes Rise: 1 hour Chill: 8 hours
Stand: 30 minutes Bake: 25 minutes
Oven: 350°F
Nutrition facts per roll: 298 cal.,
13 g fat, 21 mg chol., 258 mg sodium,
43 g carbo., 1 g fiber, 4 g pro.

1. In a large mixing bowl, combine the dry cake mix, 2 cups of the flour, the yeast and salt. Add the water and beat with an electric mixer on low speed until combined, scraping sides of bowl. Beat on high speed for 3 minutes.

2. Using a wooden spoon, stir in as much remaining flour as you can. Turn dough out onto a floured surface. Knead in enough of the remaining flour to make a smooth dough (about 3 minutes; dough will still be slightly sticky). Place dough in a large greased bowl, turning once to grease surface of dough. Cover and let rise in a warm place until double in size (about 1 hour).

3. Punch dough down. Turn dough out onto a well-floured surface and divide in half. Cover and let stand for 10 minutes. Roll each portion of dough to form a 16×9-inch rectangle.

4. Spread each rectangle with half of the ¼ cup butter. Sprinkle with a mixture of granulated sugar and cinnamon. Starting from a long side, roll up dough into a spiral. Pinch to seal. Cut the dough into 1-inch slices.

5. In a saucepan, combine the brown sugar, the 1 cup butter and corn syrup. Bring to boiling. Remove from heat. Divide mixture between two 13×9×2-inch baking pans.

6. Sprinkle walnuts evenly into the pan. Place half of the rolls, cut side down, in each baking pan. Cover and refrigerate for 8 hours or overnight.

7. Before baking, remove from refrigerator and let stand at room temperature for 30 minutes. Bake in a 350° oven about 25 minutes or until golden. Let cool for 10 minutes in pans on wire racks. Turn out onto foil. Serve warm or cool. Cover and store at room temperature for 8 hours or wrap and freeze for up to 3 months.

Coconut–Pecan Sticky Rolls

MAKES 24 ROLLS.

Des Moines Golf and Country Club Executive Chef Terry Boston took the required sticky roll and made it better with coconut and maple syrup. It's a popular addition to the lunch menu and the Sunday brunch.

3	to 3½ cups unbleached all-purpose flour or all-purpose flour
1	package active dry yeast
1	cup milk
⅓	cup granulated sugar
⅓	cup unsalted butter
½	teaspoon salt
¾	cup shredded coconut
¾	cup chopped pecans
½	cup packed brown sugar
2	teaspoons ground cinnamon
¼	cup unsalted butter
¼	cup maple-flavored syrup
½	cup orange marmalade
½	cup unsalted butter, melted

Prep: 35 minutes Rise: 1½ hours
Bake: 12 minutes Oven: 375°F
Nutrition facts per roll: 229 cal., 12 g fat, 24 mg chol., 63 mg sodium, 28 g carbo., 1 g fiber, 3 g pro.

1. In a large mixing bowl, combine 1½ cups of the flour and yeast. In a medium saucepan, heat and stir the milk, granulated sugar, the ⅓ cup butter and salt until warm (120° to 130°) and butter almost melts. Add to flour mixture. Beat with an electric mixer on low speed for 30 seconds, scraping bowl. Beat on high speed for 3 minutes. Using a wooden spoon, stir in as much of the remaining flour as you can.

2. Turn dough out onto a lightly floured surface. Knead in enough of the remaining flour to make a moderately stiff dough that's smooth and elastic (6 to 8 minutes). Shape dough into a ball. Place in a lightly greased bowl, turning once to grease the surface of the dough. Cover and let rise in a warm place until double in size (about 1 hour). Punch dough down. Divide in half. Cover and let rest for 10 minutes.

3. While dough is resting, prepare the pans. Lightly grease twenty-four 2½-inch muffin cups (use light-colored pans, if possible). In a small bowl, combine the shredded coconut, chopped pecans, brown sugar and cinnamon. Set aside. In a small saucepan, heat the ¼ cup butter and maple-flavored syrup until butter is melted. Add 1 teaspoon of this maple mixture to each muffin cup. Sprinkle with a rounded tablespoon of the coconut mixture.

4. Roll half the dough into a 12×8-inch rectangle. Thinly spread half of the orange marmalade over dough. Roll up from one of the long sides. Seal seams. Cut dough into 12 slices. Repeat with remaining dough and orange marmalade. Place 1 slice of dough in each muffin cup, cut side down. Drizzle tops evenly with the ½ cup melted butter. Cover and let rise until nearly double (about 30 minutes).

5. Bake in a 375° oven for 12 to 15 minutes or until golden brown. Cool slightly. Invert onto a serving platter. Spoon any nut mixture left in pans over rolls. Serve rolls warm.

Bonnie's Sensational Scones

MAKES 12 SCONES.

Next-door neighbor and baker extraordinaire Bonnie Swanson shared her buttery scones with Mary Beattie at Pincushion Mountain B&B. Mary took Bonnie's suggestion: use a small ice cream scoop to shape these favorites when baking them for guests.

2	cups all-purpose flour
3	tablespoons sugar
1	teaspoon ground cinnamon
½	teaspoon baking powder
⅛	teaspoon salt
½	cup butter, chilled and cut into pieces
¾	cup chopped walnuts
2	beaten eggs
⅔	cup whipping cream
1	beaten egg yolk
1	tablespoon whipping cream
	Sugar

Prep: 20 minutes Bake: 15 minutes
Cool: 5 minutes Oven: 375°F
Nutrition facts per scone: 275 cal., 19 g fat, 85 mg chol., 140 mg sodium, 22 g carbo., 1 g fiber, 5 g pro.

1. In a large bowl, combine flour, the 3 tablespoons sugar, cinnamon, baking powder and salt. Cut in butter until mixture resembles coarse crumbs. Stir in walnuts.

2. In a small bowl, combine the 2 eggs and the ⅔ cup cream. Add to the flour mixture and stir until just moistened.

3. Using a ¼-cup ice cream scoop, scoop portions of dough onto an ungreased baking sheet. Don't flatten.

4. Combine the egg yolk and 1 tablespoon whipping cream. Brush over the top of the scones. Sprinkle with additional sugar.

5. Bake in a 375° oven for 15 minutes or until scones are golden. Remove from baking sheet. Cool on wire rack for 5 minutes; serve warm.

Snow-Season Pancakes

MAKES 10 TO 12 PANCAKES.

As the snow piles up outside *Prairie Sky Guest Ranch in Veblen, South Dakota, owner Corrine Prins heats the griddle for her buttermilk pancakes that early risers can't resist. The tender, light flapjacks go down easily when topped with butter and maple syrup.*

1½	cups all-purpose flour
3	tablespoons buttermilk powder*
1	tablespoon sugar
2	teaspoons baking powder
¼	teaspoon baking soda
¼	teaspoon salt
2	beaten eggs
1¼	cups water*

Prep: 10 minutes Cook: 4 minutes/batch
Nutrition facts per pancake: 97 cal., 1 g fat, 44 mg chol., 195 mg sodium, 17 g carbo., 1 g fiber, 4 g pro.

1. In a medium bowl, combine the flour, buttermilk powder, sugar, baking powder, baking soda and salt.

2. Add the eggs and water to the flour mixture, stirring until just combined (the batter will be lumpy).

3. For each pancake, pour about ¼ cup batter onto a hot, lightly greased griddle or heavy skillet. Cook over medium heat about 2 minutes on each side or until pancakes are golden brown, turning to second sides when pancakes have bubbly surfaces and edges are slightly dry. Serve warm.

*Note: If you prefer, you can substitute 1⅓ cups buttermilk for the buttermilk powder and the water. Add the liquid buttermilk to the flour mixture with the eggs.

Very Blueberry Coffee Cake

MAKES 12 SERVINGS.

A yummy sugary crust forms on top of this berry-speckled, buttery-flavored breakfast cake from Prairie Sky Guest Ranch near Veblen, South Dakota. It's made with ingredients you likely have on hand—just pick up fresh blueberries and you're set for something special.

1½	cups sugar
½	cup butter, softened
2	eggs
1	cup milk
3	cups all-purpose flour
4	teaspoons baking powder
¼	teaspoon salt
2½	cups blueberries
2	tablespoons sugar

Prep: 20 minutes Bake: 45 minutes
Cool: 30 minutes Oven: 350°F
Nutrition facts per serving: 317 cal.,
10 g fat, 59 mg chol., 288 mg sodium,
53 g carbo., 2 g fiber, 5 g pro.

1. In a large mixing bowl, beat together the 1½ cups sugar and the butter with an electric mixer until well combined. Add eggs and beat until smooth. Gradually beat in milk on low speed (mixture may appear curdled).

2. In a medium bowl, stir together the flour, baking powder and salt. Add flour mixture to egg mixture, beating on low speed until just combined (batter will be thick). By hand, fold in 1½ cups of the blueberries.

3. Spread batter in a greased 13×9×2-inch baking pan. Sprinkle with remaining 2 tablespoons sugar and remaining berries.

4. Bake in a 350° oven about 45 minutes or until a wooden toothpick inserted into center comes out clean. Cool for 30 minutes in pan on a wire rack. Serve warm.

Spicy Pumpkin Bread

MAKES 18 SERVINGS.

Moist, spicy slices of this quick bread help awaken breakfast takers at the Inn at Pinewood near Eagle River, Wisconsin. The snipped dates and walnuts add chewiness. If you prefer, stir in your favorite dried fruit and nuts in place of the dates and walnuts.

1⅔	cups all-purpose flour
1	teaspoon baking soda
½	teaspoon salt
½	teaspoon baking powder
½	teaspoon ground cinnamon
½	teaspoon ground nutmeg
¼	teaspoon ground cloves
1½	cups sugar
1	cup canned pumpkin
½	cup water
½	cup cooking oil
2	eggs
½	cup snipped pitted dates or raisins
½	cup chopped walnuts

Prep: 20 minutes Bake: 1 hour Cool: 10 minutes
Stand: Overnight Oven: 325°F
Nutrition facts per serving: 206 cal.,
9 g fat, 24 mg chol., 154 mg sodium,
30 g carbo., 1 g fiber, 3 g pro.

1. Lightly grease a 9×5×3-inch loaf pan or three 5¾×3×2-inch loaf pans. Set the loaf pan(s) aside.

2. In a large bowl, stir together the flour, baking soda, salt, baking powder, cinnamon, nutmeg and cloves.

3. In a medium bowl, combine the sugar, pumpkin, water, cooking oil and eggs. Add to the flour mixture and stir until just combined. Fold in the dates and walnuts.

4. Turn mixture into prepared pan(s). Bake in a 325° oven for 60 minutes for the large loaf or 50 minutes for the small loaves or until a wooden toothpick inserted in the center(s) comes out clean.

5. Cool in pan(s) on a wire rack for 10 minutes. Remove from pan(s) and cool completely on wire rack. Wrap in plastic wrap and store at room temperature overnight for easier slicing. Or store in the refrigerator for up to 3 days.

Crazy-About-Cranberry Bread

Makes 16 servings.

In Cranberry country of northern Wisconsin, it's natural that you'll find the tangy fruit tucked into orange-flavored quick bread. Bill and Jane Weber make sure guests at their Inn at Pinewood in Eagle River enjoy different breads or muffins every day.

2	cups all-purpose flour
1	cup sugar
1½	teaspoons baking powder
½	teaspoon salt
¼	teaspoon baking soda
⅓	cup butter or margarine
1	beaten egg
1	teaspoon finely shredded orange peel
⅔	cup orange juice
1½	cups fresh cranberries, halved
1	cup coarsely chopped nuts

Prep: 25 minutes Bake: 1 hour Cool: 10 minutes
Stand: Overnight Oven: 350°F
Nutrition facts per serving: 198 cal., 9 g fat, 24 mg chol., 175 mg sodium, 26 g carbo., 1 g fiber, 3 g pro.

1. Lightly grease a 9×5×3-inch loaf pan, two 7½×3½×2-inch loaf pans or three 5¾×3×2-inch mini loaf pans. Set the loaf pan(s) aside.

2. In a large bowl, stir together the flour, sugar, baking powder, salt and baking soda. Cut in butter until mixture is crumbly.

3. Add the egg, orange peel and juice to the flour mixture, and stir until just combined. Fold in cranberries and nuts.

4. Turn mixture into prepared pan(s). Bake in a 350° oven for 1 hour to 1 hour and 10 minutes for the large loaf or 40 to 50 minutes for the small loaves or until a wooden toothpick inserted in center(s) comes out clean.

5. Cool in pan(s) on a wire rack for 10 minutes. Remove from pan(s) and cool the bread completely on a wire rack. Wrap in plastic wrap and store at room temperature overnight for easier slicing. Or store in the refrigerator for up to 3 days.

Best-Ever Rolls

MAKES 24 ROLLS.

These golden rolls from Prairie Sky Guest Ranch near Veblen, South Dakota, fit in with any meal. Owner Corrine Prins even uses them for sandwiches. "I got this recipe from my mom 30 years ago," Corrine says. "She makes the best buns!"

2	cups milk
½	cup sugar
⅓	cup butter or margarine
2	teaspoons salt
2	packages active dry yeast
⅓	cup warm water (105°F to 115°F)
8	to 9 cups all-purpose flour
3	beaten eggs
	Butter or margarine, melted

Prep: 45 minutes Rise: 1½ hours
Bake: 18 minutes Oven: 375°F
Nutrition facts per roll: 209 cal., 5 g fat, 38 mg chol., 250 mg sodium, 35 g carbo., 1 g fiber, 6 g pro.

1. In a medium saucepan, heat the milk, sugar, ⅓ cup butter and salt until butter almost melts. Remove the saucepan from heat. Cool to lukewarm (105° to 115°).

2. In a small bowl, dissolve the yeast in the warm water. Let stand until bubbly.

3. In a large mixing bowl, combine 3 cups of the flour and the milk mixture. Beat with an electric mixer on low speed for 30 seconds, scraping sides of bowl constantly. Add the yeast mixture and beat on high speed for 3 minutes. Beat in the eggs.

4. Using a wooden spoon, stir in as much remaining flour as you can. Turn out onto a lightly floured surface. Knead in enough of the remaining flour to form a moderately soft dough that is smooth and elastic (3 to 5 minutes total).

5. Place dough in a greased bowl; turn once to grease surface of the dough. Cover and let rise in a warm place until double in size (about 1 hour).

6. Punch dough down. Turn dough out onto a lightly floured surface. Divide dough in half. Cover and let rest for 10 minutes. Divide dough into 24 portions; shape into buns.

7. Place on lightly greased baking sheets. Or place in two lightly greased 13×9×2-inch baking pans. Cover and let rise until nearly double (about 30 minutes).

8. Bake in a 375° oven for 18 to 20 minutes or until golden brown. Transfer to a wire rack to cool. Brush with melted butter while warm.

French Dressing
with Pizzazz

MAKES 2½ CUPS, TWENTY (2–TABLESPOON) SERVINGS.

This sweet-style homemade salad dressing starts with tomato soup. Sugar, vinegar and seasonings give it enough zip to make the menu of the Overlook Restaurant near Leavenworth, Indiana.

1	10¾-ounce can condensed tomato soup
1	cup sugar
⅔	cup salad oil
¼	cup vinegar
1	teaspoon celery seeds
1	teaspoon Worcestershire sauce
½	teaspoon garlic salt
½	teaspoon onion powder
½	teaspoon dry mustard
½	teaspoon paprika

Start to Finish: 10 minutes

Nutrition facts per 2 tablespoons: 112 cal., 8 g fat, 0 mg chol., 133 mg sodium, 12 g carbo., 0 g fiber, 0 g pro.

1. In a medium bowl, combine all ingredients. Whisk until combined.

2. Serve immediately, or cover and store in the refrigerator for up to 2 weeks. Stir before serving.

Senior Open House Salad

The 1999 U.S. Senior Open drew 253,000 people to the Des Moines Golf and Country Club in West Des Moines. The largest country club in Iowa is located on 500 acres of rolling hills. When served at dinner, this house salad includes Parmesan breadsticks.

5	cups torn mixed salad greens
2	medium tomatoes, cut into wedges
½	cup thinly sliced cucumber
	House Dressing
½	cup purchased seasoned croutons

Prep: 20 minutes Chill: Up to 1 week
Nutrition facts per serving: 187 cal., 15 g fat, 11 mg chol., 268 mg sodium, 9 g carbo., 2 g fiber, 2 g pro.

1. For salad greens: In a large bowl of cold water, immerse the salad greens. After a few minutes, lift out the greens. Immerse the greens again, if necessary, to remove any dirt or sand particles. Discard the water. Drain the greens in a colander. Place the greens on a clean kitchen towel or several layers of paper towels; gently pat dry. (Or use a salad spinner to spin the greens dry.) Wrap dried greens in a dry kitchen towel or paper towels; refrigerate for at least 1 hour or up to several hours to crisp. In a large salad bowl, toss together the salad greens, tomatoes and cucumber.

2. Stir the House Dressing well; pour dressing over the salad mixture. Toss lightly. Sprinkle with croutons; toss to mix.

House Dressing: In a small bowl, combine 1 cup mayonnaise, ½ cup creamy garlic salad dressing, ½ cup dairy sour cream, ½ teaspoon Worcestershire sauce, ⅛ teaspoon salt, ⅛ teaspoon garlic powder and ⅛ teaspoon ground white pepper. Cover and store in the refrigerator for up to 1 week. If necessary, stir in 1 to 2 tablespoons milk to make desired consistency. Makes 2 cups.

Maple Bluff Salad

MAKES 6 TO 8 SIDE-DISH SALADS.

From the dining room of Maple Bluff Country Club in Madison, Wisconsin, members can look out on the course's venerable maples, oaks and hickories. If they're smart, they choose this autumn specialty from Executive Chef Gary Jacobson.

10	cups mesclun (mixed baby greens) or torn mixed greens
½	medium apple or pear, peeled, cored and coarsely chopped
2	tablespoons apple cider or apple juice
2	tablespoons balsamic vinegar
2	tablespoons cider vinegar
1	shallot, coarsely chopped
1	clove garlic, minced
⅛	teaspoon salt
2	teaspoons Dijon-style mustard
¼	cup salad oil
½	pound potatoes (sweet potatoes, yams, Yukon Gold, russet or long white), peeled
	Cooking oil or shortening for deep-fat frying
	Five-spice powder
½	cup roasted and salted shelled pumpkin seeds or coarsely chopped peanuts

Prep: 20 minutes Cool: 30 minutes Chill: 1 hour
Fry: 1½ minutes/batch
Nutrition facts per serving: 285 cal., 23 g fat, 0 mg chol., 183 mg sodium, 16 g carbo., 3 g fiber, 8 g pro.

1. For salad greens: In a large bowl of cold water, immerse the salad greens. After a few minutes, lift out the greens. Immerse the greens again, if necessary, to remove any dirt or sand particles. Discard the water. Drain the greens in a colander. Place the greens on a clean kitchen towel or several layers of paper towels; gently pat dry. (Or use a salad spinner to spin the greens dry.) Wrap dried greens in a dry kitchen towel or paper towels; refrigerate for at least 1 hour or up to several hours to crisp.

2. For vinaigrette: In a small saucepan, combine apple, apple cider, vinegars, shallot, garlic and salt. Bring to boiling; reduce heat. Simmer, uncovered, over medium heat for 6 to 8 minutes or until mixture is reduced to a scant ½ cup, stirring often. Remove from heat; cool to room temperature, about 30 minutes.

3. In a small food processor bowl or blender container, place the cooled vinaigrette mixture and mustard. Cover and process or blend until smooth. With processor or blender running, add oil in a thin steady stream. (As necessary, stop processor and scrape down sides of bowl.) Cover and refrigerate vinaigrette at least 1 hour before serving.

4. Cut the potatoes into slices about 2 inches long and ¼ inch thick. Stack the slices and cut them lengthwise into strips ³⁄₁₆ to ¼ inch wide.

5. In a heavy, deep 3-quart saucepan or deep-fat fryer heat 1½ inches oil or shortening to 365°. Using a spoon, carefully add the potato strips, a few at a time, to hot oil. Fry for 1½ to 2½ minutes or until brown, turning once. Using a slotted spoon, remove potatoes from hot oil. Drain on paper towels. Lightly sprinkle with five-spice powder; set aside. (Don't fry too many potatoes at one time because oil will foam when the potatoes are added.)

6. To serve, place the salad greens in a large salad bowl. Stir the vinaigrette; pour over the greens. Lightly toss. Arrange salad greens on chilled salad plates. Top each salad with potato strips and pumpkin seeds. Serve immediately.

Oven-Roasted Root Vegetables

MAKES 4 SIDE-DISH SERVINGS.

Roasting gives vegetables deep, vibrant color and rich flavor, and adding rutabagas to the mix brings a little more intrigue to the dish. Serve this roasted winter vegetable quartet alongside Braised Lamb Shanks (see recipe, page 91).

2	medium parsnips, peeled, quartered and cut into ½-inch slices
½	medium rutabaga, peeled and cut into ½-inch cubes
1	cup packaged peeled baby carrots or 2 medium carrots, halved lengthwise and cut into 2-inch pieces
1	cup pearl onions, peeled*, or 1 medium red onion, cut into wedges
2	tablespoons olive oil Salt and black pepper

Prep: 20 minutes Bake: 1 hour 10 minutes
Oven: 350°F
Nutrition facts per serving: 116 cal., 7 g fat, 0 mg chol., 167 mg sodium, 13 g carbo., 4 g fiber, 1 g pro.

1. In a 9×9×2-inch baking pan combine parsnips, rutabaga, carrots and pearl onions. Drizzle olive oil over vegetables. Lightly season with salt and pepper; toss to coat. Bake, covered, in a 350° oven for 45 minutes. Uncover and stir the vegetables. Bake, uncovered, for 25 to 30 minutes more or until vegetables are starting to brown, stirring occasionally.

*Note: For easier peeling, blanch pearl onions in boiling water for 1 minute. Drain and cool. Cut a thin slice from root end of onion and slip onion from skin.

Roasted Garlic Whipped Potatoes

MAKES 4 SERVINGS.

Mashed potatoes take on a whole new dimension with the addition of roasted garlic. Each bite is a forkful of heaven. The Bellerive Country Club of St. Louis serves these with Braised Lamb Shanks (see recipe, page 91).

4	large baking potatoes (6 to 8 ounces each)
½	cup half-and-half or light cream
¼	cup unsalted butter
1	tablespoon bottled minced roasted garlic
	Salt and ground white pepper

Prep: 10 minutes Cook: 20 minutes
Stand: 5 minutes

Nutrition facts per serving: 254 cal., 16 g fat, 44 mg chol., 167 mg sodium, 26 g carbo., 2 g fiber, 4 g pro.

1. Peel and quarter potatoes. Cook, covered, in a small amount of boiling lightly salted water for 20 to 25 minutes or until tender; drain. Meanwhile, in a small saucepan, combine half-and-half and butter. Heat over low heat until butter melts. Remove from heat. Stir in roasted garlic. Let stand, covered, for 5 minutes. Strain, if you like (mixture may appear curdled).

2. Mash drained potatoes with a potato masher or beat with an electric mixer. Gradually beat in butter mixture to make potatoes light and fluffy. Season to taste with salt and white pepper.

Roadhouse-Style Vegetables

MAKES 6 SERVINGS.

Oakland Hills Country Club in Bloomfield, Michigan, usually serves these buttery vegetables alongside Lake Perch with Roadhouse Sauce (see recipe, page 94). Try them the next time you pan-fry or grill steak.

2   large baking potatoes
       (6 to 8 ounces each)
1   large fennel bulb
2   cups packaged peeled
       baby carrots
2   medium leeks, sliced
2   bay leaves
2   tablespoons butter, melted
       Salt and black pepper

Prep: 15 minutes Cook: 6 minutes
Nutrition facts per serving: 110 cal., 4 g fat, 11 mg chol., 92 mg sodium, 17 g carbo., 6 g fiber, 2 g pro.

1. Peel and thinly slice potatoes. Remove any tough or bruised outer leaves from fennel bulb. Trim off the root end and the stems; discard. Thoroughly rinse the trimmed bulb. Halve the fennel bulb lengthwise and remove the core. Cut the bulb crosswise into thin slices.

2. In a 4-quart Dutch oven, bring a small amount of lightly salted water to boiling. Add the potatoes, fennel, carrots, leeks, and bay leaves. Return to boiling; reduce heat. Simmer, covered, for 6 to 8 minutes or just until vegetables are crisp-tender.

3. Drain well; discard bay leaves. Drizzle melted butter over vegetables; toss to coat evenly. Season to taste with salt and pepper. Serve warm.

Pheasant Breast Supreme

MAKES 4 SERVINGS.

Since South Dakota is said to be the "Pheasant Capital of the World," it makes sense to have this pheasant entrée on the menu at the Minnehaha Country Club in Sioux Falls, says Executive Chef Dirk Peterson.

4	medium skinless, boneless pheasant or chicken breast halves (1 pound total)
¼	cup all-purpose flour
⅛	teaspoon salt
⅛	teaspoon black pepper
3	tablespoons butter
½	cup sliced fresh mushrooms
¼	cup finely chopped shallots
¼	cup finely chopped celery
¼	cup cream sherry or chicken broth
2	teaspoons finely shredded lemon peel
3	tablespoons lemon juice
½	cup chicken broth
1	cup whipping cream
¼	cup dairy sour cream
2	tablespoons butter
2	cloves garlic, minced
6	cups torn fresh spinach
¼	cup toasted sliced almonds

Start to Finish: 55 minutes
Nutrition facts per serving: 639 cal., 48 g fat, 194 mg chol., 455 mg sodium, 15 g carbo., 6 g fiber, 35 g pro.

1. Place a pheasant or chicken breast half, boned side up, between 2 pieces of plastic wrap. Working from the center to edges, very gently pound pheasant or chicken breast half with the flat side of a meat mallet to ⅛ inch thick. Remove plastic wrap. Repeat with the remaining pheasant or chicken.

2. In a shallow dish, stir together flour, salt and pepper. Lightly coat pheasant or chicken on both sides with flour mixture; shake off excess.

3. In a large skillet, melt 2 tablespoons of the butter. Cook pheasant or chicken, half at a time, over medium heat for 3 to 4 minutes until no longer pink, turning occasionally. Remove from skillet and keep warm.

4. In the same skillet, add the remaining 1 tablespoon butter. Cook mushrooms, shallots and celery in hot butter for 5 to 6 minutes or until tender, stirring often. Carefully add the cream sherry, lemon peel and juice. Using a wooden spoon, stir and scrape up browned bits in skillet.

5. Add the ½ cup chicken broth. Bring to boiling; reduce heat. Cook, uncovered, over medium-high heat for 6 to 8 minutes or until liquid is reduced to about 2 tablespoons, stirring often. Whisk in the whipping cream and sour cream. Cook, whisking constantly, over medium heat for 5 minutes or until mixture thickens and is reduced to about 1 cup. Return pheasant or chicken pieces to skillet; heat through.

6. In a 12-inch skillet, melt the remaining 2 tablespoons butter. Add garlic. Cook garlic for 1 minute. Add the spinach. Using two spoons or tongs, toss 30 seconds or until spinach is coated and just wilted.

7. To serve, divide spinach among 4 dinner plates. Place a pheasant breast on each bed of spinach and pour sauce over all. Sprinkle with almonds.

Signature Room Pork Chop

MAKES 4 SERVINGS.

The John Hancock Center in Chicago is one of the tallest buildings in the world. It's an awesome experience to dine at the Signature Room on the 95th floor, savoring the view and this juicy chop served on a bed of lentils with apples and corn.

4 pork loin chops or rib chops, cut 1½ inches thick (about 2½ pounds total)

¼ cup Barbecue Dry Rub

2 cups apple, orange, pecan or peach wood chips

1 cup dry red lentils

1 14-ounce can vegetable or chicken broth (1¾ cups)

2 tablespoons olive oil

1 large Granny Smith apple, peeled, cored and chopped

¼ cup fresh corn kernels

½ teaspoon salt

¼ teaspoon freshly ground black pepper

Salt and black pepper

⅓ cup bottled barbecue sauce

3 tablespoons molasses

4 teaspoons brown sugar

1 tablespoon bourbon or apple juice

Prep: 35 minutes Marinate: 30 minutes
Grill: 35 minutes
Nutrition facts per serving: 676 cal., 19 g fat, 127 mg chol., 1,666 mg sodium, 58 g carbo., 9 g fiber, 64 g pro.

1. Trim fat from chops. Sprinkle Barbecue Dry Rub evenly over chops; rub in with your fingers. Cover and marinate at room temperature for 30 minutes or in the refrigerator for 4 to 24 hours. At least 1 hour before grilling, soak wood chips in enough water to cover. Drain before using.

2. In a covered grill, arrange medium-hot coals around a drip pan. Test for medium heat above pan*. Sprinkle the drained wood chips over coals. Place chops on grill rack over drip pan. Cover and smoke for 35 to 40 minutes or until juices run clear.

3. Rinse lentils under cold running water, lifting lentils with your fingers to clean. In a medium saucepan, place lentils and vegetable broth. Bring to boiling; reduce heat. Simmer, covered, for 10 minutes or until lentils are tender and liquid is absorbed; set aside.

4. In a large saucepan, heat oil over medium heat. Add chopped apple, corn, ½ teaspoon salt and ¼ teaspoon pepper. Cook and stir for 3 minutes or until apples are just tender. Stir in lentils; heat through. Season to taste with additional salt and pepper.

5. For barbecue sauce: In a small saucepan, combine bottled barbecue sauce, molasses, brown sugar and bourbon. Bring to boiling; reduce heat. Simmer, uncovered, for 5 minutes or to desired consistency. To serve, spoon lentil mixture onto 4 dinner plates. Place a pork chop on top of each lentil portion. Drizzle with barbecue sauce.

Barbecue Dry Rub: In a small bowl, stir together 2 tablespoons sugar, 2 tablespoons garlic powder, 2 tablespoons paprika, 1 tablespoon kosher salt, 1 tablespoon onion powder, 1 tablespoon ground cumin, 1 tablespoon ground coriander and 1 tablespoon chili powder. Store rub in a covered container up to 6 months. Makes about ⅔ cup rub (enough for about 5 pounds meat or poultry).

*Note: To test for medium heat, you should be able to hold your hand over the heat at the height of the food for 4 seconds.

Braised Lamb Shanks

MAKES 4 SERVINGS.

Founded in 1897, Bellerive Country Club of St. Louis dishes out great golf. Not to be outdone, the kitchen serves this savory lamb main dish that's slow-cooked to tender perfection with wine and vegetables.

4	meaty lamb shanks (about 2½ pounds total)
2	tablespoons olive oil
2	large carrots, coarsely chopped
2	celery stalks, coarsely chopped
1	large onion, coarsely chopped
2	cups port wine
1	cup dry red wine
4	sprigs fresh thyme
4	cloves garlic, halved
2	tablespoons whole black peppercorns
4	cups veal, chicken or vegetable broth
2	tomatoes, coarsely chopped
2	tablespoons unsalted butter
	Roasted Garlic Whipped Potatoes, (page 86) (optional)
	Oven-Roasted Root Vegetables, (page 85) (optional)

Prep: 15 minutes Bake: 1½ hours
Cook: 40 minutes Oven: 350°F
Nutrition facts per serving: 629 cal., 30 g fat, 111 mg chol., 1,257 mg sodium, 22 g carbo., 1 g fiber, 29 g pro.

1. Season shanks on all sides with salt and black pepper. In a 4- to 6-quart Dutch oven, heat oil over medium-high heat. Add lamb shanks and brown on all sides. Remove shanks; set aside.

2. Add the carrots, celery and onion to the same pan. Cook over medium heat for 10 to 12 minutes or until vegetables are brown, stirring occasionally. Add the port and red wine. Bring to boiling; reduce heat. Boil gently, uncovered, for 10 minutes.

3. Place the thyme sprigs, garlic and peppercorns in the center of a 6-inch square of several layers of 100-percent-cotton cheesecloth. Bring the cheesecloth up around the spices. Using a cotton string, tie cheesecloth to form a bag. Trim excess cloth.

4. Add browned lamb shanks, cheesecloth bag, broth and tomatoes to the wine mixture. Bring to boiling. Remove from heat. Cover and roast in a 350° oven for 1½ to 2 hours or until meat is tender. Remove lamb shanks from pan; set aside and keep warm. Strain cooking liquid. Discard the vegetables and cheesecloth bag. Skim fat from liquid.

5. For sauce: Return the reserved liquid to the Dutch oven. Bring to boiling; reduce heat. Boil gently, uncovered, until liquid is reduced to about 3 cups, about 10 to 12 minutes. Whisk butter, 1 tablespoon at a time, into liquid.

6. To serve: If you like, spoon Roasted Garlic Whipped Potatoes in the middle of 4 shallow soup bowls. Place 1 lamb shank next to potatoes. If you like, spoon some of the Oven-Roasted Root Vegetables around the potatoes. Pour some of the sauce over each serving.

Note: Remaining sauce can be stored in the refrigerator for up to 3 days or in the freezer for up to 3 months and used as a soup or gravy base. For a nonalcoholic version, substitute beef broth for the port and red wine.

Unbelievable Les Bourgeois Beef

Diners at Les Bourgeois Winegarden and Bistro near Rocheport, Missouri, can almost forget their knives when eating this tender beef draped with sauce. The chef serves Gorgonzola mashed potatoes with this specialty, but you can choose your favorite potatoes.

⅓   cup dried mushrooms, such as morels or chanterelles (¼ ounce)
3   tablespoons butter
1   cup chopped red onion
1   tablespoon whole green peppercorns in brine, drained
2   teaspoons cracked black pepper
1   cup dry Marsala or dry red wine
2   cups whipping cream
½   cup condensed beef broth
    Salt
8   beef tenderloin steaks, cut 1¼ inches thick

Prep: 5 minutes Stand: 20 minutes
Cook: 43 minutes Grill: 14 minutes
Nutrition facts per serving: 525 cal., 37 g fat, 181 mg chol., 253 mg sodium, 8 g carbo., 1 g fiber, 32 g pro.

1. For sauce: In a small bowl, cover the dried mushrooms with hot water. Let stand for 20 minutes. Rinse under warm running water and squeeze out the excess moisture. Chop mushrooms.

2. In large skillet, melt the butter over medium heat. Add the mushrooms, onion, drained green peppercorns and cracked black pepper. Cook, uncovered, over medium-low heat for 15 minutes, stirring frequently.

3. Add Marsala. Bring to boiling; reduce heat. Simmer, uncovered, for 8 to 10 minutes or until wine is reduced by about half and mushroom mixture is slightly thickened, stirring occasionally.

4. Add whipping cream and condensed beef broth. Cook over medium heat just until tiny bubbles form around the edge; reduce heat. Cook over medium-low heat, stirring occasionally with a wooden spoon, for 20 to 25 minutes or until mixture thickens to desired consistency. Season to taste with salt; set aside.

5. For tenderloin steaks: Trim fat from steaks. Grill steaks on the rack of an uncovered grill directly over medium coals to desired doneness, turning once halfway through. Allow 14 to 18 minutes for medium rare (145°) and 18 to 22 minutes for medium (160°).

6. To serve, reheat the Marsala sauce; transfer to a serving bowl and pass with steaks. Serve with your favorite mashed potatoes and green beans, if you like.

Lake Perch
with Roadhouse Sauce

MAKES 6 SERVINGS.

The world comes to the Oakland Hills Country Club in Bloomfield, Michigan, for the 2004 Ryder Cup international tournament. If they're fortunate, golfers and fans can savor this Midwest dish where seasoned buttermilk flavors lake perch draped in a wine sauce.

6	fresh or frozen lake perch, cod or flounder fillets, about ½ inch thick (5 to 6 ounces each)
1	cup buttermilk or sour milk*
1	tablespoon snipped fresh parsley
2	teaspoons snipped fresh chives
1	teaspoon minced shallot
1	teaspoon minced garlic
½	teaspoon salt
¼	teaspoon ground white pepper
	Roadhouse Sauce
	Roadhouse-Style Vegetables (page 87) (optional)
⅔	cup all-purpose flour
½	teaspoon paprika
½	teaspoon black pepper
¼	cup unsalted butter

Prep: 25 minutes Marinate: 20 minutes
Fry: 4 minutes/batch Oven: 300°F
Nutrition facts per serving: 437 cal., 29 g fat, 204 mg chol., 351 mg sodium, 13 g carbo., 1 g fiber, 30 g pro.

1. Thaw fish, if frozen. Rinse fish; pat dry. For marinade: In a large baking dish, combine buttermilk, parsley, chives, shallot, garlic, salt and white pepper. Add fish; turn to coat. Cover and marinate at room temperature for 20 minutes (or in the refrigerator for 2 hours), turning fillets occasionally. Prepare Roadhouse Sauce and, if you like, Roadhouse-Style Vegetables.

2. On a sheet of waxed paper in a pie plate or a shallow dish, combine flour, paprika and black pepper. Remove fish fillets from marinade; drain. Discard the marinade. Coat both sides of each fillet with flour mixture; shake off excess flour.

3. In a large nonstick skillet, melt 2 tablespoons of the butter. Add half of the fish in a single layer. (If fillets have skin, fry skin side last.) Fry fish over medium-high heat on one side for 2 to 4 minutes or until golden. Turn carefully. Fry for 2 to 4 minutes more or until golden and fish flakes easily when tested with a fork. Drain on paper towels. Keep warm in a 300° oven while frying remaining fish in remaining butter.

4. To serve, place each fish fillet on a warmed dinner plate. If you like, arrange some of the Roadhouse-Style Vegetables next to fish. Serve with Roadhouse Sauce.

Roadhouse Sauce: In a large skillet, combine ¼ cup dry white wine or chicken broth, ¼ cup water, 2 tablespoons lemon juice, 1 teaspoon minced shallots, ½ teaspoon minced garlic and ⅛ teaspoon kosher or sea salt. Bring to boiling; reduce heat. Simmer, uncovered, for 5 to 8 minutes or until reduced to a scant ¼ cup. Whisk in 3 tablespoons whipping cream. Simmer, uncovered, for 1½ to 2 minutes more or until reduced to about ¼ cup. Reduce heat to low. Whisk in ½ cup unsalted cold butter (no substitutes), 1 tablespoon at a time. Season to taste. Serve warm.

**Note*: For 1 cup of sour milk, place 1 tablespoon of lemon juice or vinegar in a 1-cup glass measuring cup. Add enough milk to measure 1 cup; stir until combined. Let stand 5 minutes before using.

Cardamom Sea Bass

Classic elegance prevails at Brookside Country Club in Canton, Ohio, established in 1920. Executive Chef Kenneth J. Bucholtz finishes this cardamom-flour coated fish with a mango-orange relish.

6   fresh or frozen skinless sea bass, trout, orange roughy or cod fillets, about ½ inch thick (7 to 8 ounces each)

⅔   cup all-purpose flour

2   teaspoons ground cardamom

¼   cup butter

     Mango-Orange Relish

12   fresh chive stems

Prep: 20 minutes Chill: 2 hours
Fry: 6 minutes/batch Oven: 300°F
Nutrition facts per serving: 361 cal., 12 g fat, 103 mg chol., 220 mg sodium, 21 g carbo., 2 g fiber, 39 g pro.

1. Thaw fish, if frozen. Rinse fish; pat dry.

2. On a sheet of waxed paper in a pie plate or a shallow dish, combine flour and cardamom. Coat both sides of each fillet with the flour mixture; shake off excess flour.

3. In a 12-inch skillet, preferably nonstick, melt 2 tablespoons of the butter. Add 2 or 3 of the fish fillets in a single layer. Fry fish over medium-high heat on one side for 2 to 4 minutes or until golden. Turn carefully. Fry about 4 minutes more or until golden and fish flakes easily when tested with a fork. Drain on paper towels. Keep warm in a 300° oven while frying remaining fish in remaining butter, if necessary.

4. To serve, place a fish fillet on a warm serving plate. Spoon Mango-Orange Relish on top of the fillet. Garnish with chives.

Mango-Orange Relish: To prepare a mango, slide a sharp knife next to the seed along one side of the mango, cutting through the fruit. Repeat on the other side of the seed to divide into two large pieces. Then cut away all of the mango that remains around the seed. Remove all of the peel and chop the mango. In a medium bowl, combine the chopped mango; 2 medium oranges, peeled and sectioned; ½ cup chopped bottled roasted red sweet pepper; ⅓ cup orange juice; 2 tablespoons dry white wine and 1 tablespoon snipped fresh cilantro. Cover and chill for 2 to 4 hours before serving. Makes about 2⅓ cups relish.

Kristofer's Crabmeat Whitefish

MAKES 8 SERVINGS.

Terri Milligan, chef at the Inn at Kristofer's in Sister Bay, Wisconsin, adds seasoned crabmeat and a Marsala Sauce to Lake Michigan whitefish for an unforgettable entrée. Between the food and the view, it's hard to tell which is more inspiring.

8	7- to 8-ounce fresh or frozen skinless whitefish, orange roughy or red snapper fillets (3⅓ to 4 pounds total)
	Marsala Sauce
½	cup chopped onion
3	cloves garlic, minced
2	tablespoons butter
2	cups sliced fresh mushrooms
1	cup chopped red sweet pepper
½	cup dry white wine
¾	teaspoon fennel seeds, crushed
½	teaspoon salt
½	teaspoon dried dillweed
½	teaspoon dried thyme, crushed
¼	teaspoon black pepper
2	cups panko (Japanese bread crumbs) or fine dry bread crumbs
1	6½-ounce can lump crabmeat, drained, flaked, cartilage removed
¼	cup butter, melted

Prep: 45 minutes   Bake: 25 minutes   Oven: 350°F
Nutrition facts per serving: 698 cal., 43 g fat, 240 mg chol., 516 mg sodium, 19 g carbo., 2 g fiber, 47 g pro.

1. Thaw fish, if frozen. Rinse fish; pat dry. Cut fish fillets in half crosswise. Cover; refrigerate until ready to stuff. Prepare Marsala Sauce. Cover surface of sauce with plastic wrap and set aside.

2. For stuffing: In a large skillet, cook onion and garlic in the 2 tablespoons hot butter until onion is tender. Add mushrooms, sweet pepper, wine, fennel seeds, salt, dillweed, thyme and black pepper. Bring to boiling; reduce heat. Boil gently, uncovered, about 6 minutes or until most of liquid has evaporated and vegetables are tender. Cool slightly.

3. In a food processor bowl, place mushroom mixture. Cover and process with several on/off turns until coarsely chopped. (Don't chop mixture too finely.) Transfer mixture to a large bowl. Add panko and crabmeat. Stir to combine. (If necessary, add a small amount of water to moisten.)

4. Line a 15×10×1-inch baking pan with foil. Lightly spray foil with nonstick cooking spray. Arrange 8 of the largest pieces of fish on prepared pan. Spoon about ½ cup of stuffing on each fillet. For each stack, place one of the smaller pieces of fish on top of stuffing, skinned side up. Drizzle with some of the melted butter. Bake in a 350° oven for 25 to 30 minutes or until an instant-read thermometer inserted into stuffing registers 165° and fish flakes easily when tested with a fork. Meanwhile, reheat Marsala Sauce. To serve, place a fish stack on a dinner plate. Drizzle with Marsala Sauce.

Marsala Sauce: In a heavy medium saucepan, bring 1 cup dry Marsala or dry red wine and 2 finely chopped shallots to boiling; reduce heat. Boil gently, uncovered, for 7 minutes. Strain mixture, reserve wine. Discard shallots. Return wine to saucepan. Bring to boiling; reduce heat. Boil gently, uncovered, until reduced to ½ cup. Add 2 cups whipping cream, ¼ cup chopped green onions, ½ teaspoon dried dillweed and ½ teaspoon dried thyme, crushed. Bring to boiling; reduce heat. Boil gently until mixture is reduced to 1½ cups, stirring constantly. Season with salt and pepper.

Perfect for everyday dinner yet

hardly mundane fare, these one-dish

recipes will delight. Soups, stews

and skillet meals—each bite warms and

One-Dish Delights

comforts the soul. Perhaps best of all,

they're easy on the cook and the dishwasher.

Chicken Dinner in a Packet, page 114

Town and Country Wild Rice Soup

MAKES 8 SERVINGS.

A Minnesota staple—nutty and chewy wild rice—stars in this creamy soup. Note that wild rice isn't truly rice at all; it's a long-grain marsh grass native to the northern Great Lakes area. No matter, it's delicious.

½	cup wild rice
⅓	cup finely chopped carrot
⅓	cup finely chopped onion
⅓	cup finely chopped celery
1	tablespoon butter
4	cups chicken broth
12	ounces skinless, boneless chicken breast halves, cut into ¾-inch pieces
¼	cup all-purpose flour
¼	cup butter, softened
4	cups whipping cream, half-and-half or light cream
	Salt and black pepper

Prep: 30 minutes Cook: 40 minutes
Nutrition facts per serving: 341 cal., 23 g fat, 89 mg chol., 728 mg sodium, 17 g carbo., 1 g fiber, 16 g pro.

1. In a fine wire mesh strainer, rinse the wild rice under cold running water, lifting the rice with your fingers to clean thoroughly; drain. Set aside.

2. In a Dutch oven, cook carrot, onion and celery in the 1 tablespoon butter over medium heat for 5 minutes or until vegetables are tender, but not brown. Add the wild rice and chicken broth. Bring to boiling; reduce heat. Simmer, covered, for 20 minutes. Add chicken pieces; simmer 20 to 25 minutes more or until the wild rice is tender.

3. In a small bowl, whisk together the flour and butter to make a smooth paste.

4. In the Dutch oven, stir the flour mixture into the rice and chicken mixture. Cook and stir until thickened and bubbly. Cook and stir for 1 minute more. Add the whipping cream. Cook over medium heat, stirring frequently, until the mixture is heated through. Season to taste with salt and pepper.

Tomato Soup
with Dumplings

MAKES 4 SERVINGS.

Remember Grandma's dumpling soup? Here's an update. Basil-flecked dumplings are simmered on top of this pureed veggie and tomato soup. It's such a fresh-tasting soup, you can enjoy it any season.

1	cup coarsely chopped onion
1	shallot, chopped
1	clove garlic, chopped
2	tablespoons olive oil
1	14-ounce can reduced-sodium chicken broth
½	cup coarsely chopped carrot
½	cup coarsely chopped celery
½	cup coarsely chopped red sweet pepper
1	tablespoon lemon juice
½	teaspoon sugar
1½	pounds ripe plum tomatoes, peeled, seeded and finely chopped (about 2 cups)
1	tablespoon gin (optional)
	Basil Dumplings
	Salt and freshly ground black pepper
	Snipped fresh basil

Prep: 35 minutes Cook: 35 minutes
Nutrition facts per serving: 124 cal., 7 g fat, 35 mg chol., 214 mg sodium, 13 g carbo., 2 g fiber, 4 g pro.

1. In a large saucepan, cook onion, shallot and garlic in olive oil over medium heat about 5 minutes or until onion is tender, stirring frequently. Add broth, carrot, celery, sweet pepper, lemon juice and sugar. Bring to boiling; reduce heat. Simmer, covered, for 20 to 25 minutes or until vegetables are very tender. Cool slightly (don't drain).

2. In a food processor bowl or blender container, process or blend the mixture, half at a time, until smooth.

3. Return the pureed mixture to the same saucepan. Add the tomatoes and the gin, if you like. Cook, uncovered, over low heat for 10 minutes or until soup is heated through, stirring often.

4. Meanwhile, prepare Basil Dumplings. Fill a Dutch oven half full with water; bring to boiling. Drop dumpling dough from a slightly rounded ½-teaspoon measuring spoon into boiling water and cook for 4 to 5 minutes (start timing after dough rises to the surface) or until cooked through, turning once. To test for doneness, remove a dumpling and check the center, making sure it's cooked through. Using a slotted spoon, remove the dumplings and drain in a colander. Rinse dumplings under cold running water; drain again.

5. Add dumplings to soup in saucepan; heat through. Season to taste with salt and black pepper. Garnish each serving with snipped basil.

Basil Dumplings: In a small bowl, combine ⅓ cup all-purpose flour, 2 teaspoons snipped fresh basil and ¼ teaspoon baking powder. Combine 1 beaten egg and 2 teaspoons cooking oil; pour all at once into flour mixture. Using a wooden spoon, beat until a soft, sticky dough forms.

Tortellini Chowder

MAKES 6 TO 8 SERVINGS.

Italian-style tortellini and *Mexican seasonings combine in this delight from Palmer's Deli & Market in Urbandale, Iowa. Make it as spicy as you like with the ground red pepper and chile peppers. For a little extra kick, don't seed the jalapeño.*

2	cups refrigerated or frozen cheese-filled tortellini
⅔	cup chopped onion
½	cup chopped red sweet pepper
⅓	cup chopped fresh green chile pepper * (Anaheim or poblano)
2	tablespoons minced garlic
1	fresh jalapeño pepper *, seeded and chopped (1 tablespoon)
1	tablespoon butter or margarine
3	cups chicken broth
2	cups cubed peeled potatoes
1	teaspoon ground cumin
⅛	teaspoon ground red pepper
2	tablespoons all-purpose flour
2	tablespoons butter or margarine, melted
1	15¼-ounce can whole-kernel corn, drained
2	cups half-and-half or light cream
	Fried Corn Tortilla Strips or broken tortilla chips (optional)

Prep: 30 minutes Cook: 25 minutes
Nutrition facts per serving: 463 cal., 21 g fat, 46 mg chol., 1,073 mg sodium, 55 g carbo., 3 g fiber, 16 g pro.

1. Cook cheese-filled tortellini according to package directions. Drain; set aside.

2. In a Dutch oven, cook the onion, red sweet pepper, green chile pepper, garlic and jalapeño pepper in the 1 tablespoon butter about 5 minutes or until vegetables are tender, but not brown.

3. Carefully stir in broth, potatoes, cumin, ¼ teaspoon salt, ¼ teaspoon black pepper and the ground red pepper. Bring to boiling; reduce heat. Simmer, covered, for 25 to 30 minutes or until potatoes are just tender.

4. In a small bowl, stir together flour and the 2 tablespoons melted butter; add to soup mixture. Cook and stir over medium heat until thickened and bubbly. Cook and stir for 1 minute.

5. Reduce heat and add tortellini, corn, and half-and-half. Heat through. Ladle into warm soup bowls. Top with Fried Corn Tortilla Strips or broken tortilla chips, if you like.

Fried Corn Tortilla Strips: Cut 6 corn tortillas in half, then cut them crosswise into ½-inch-wide strips. In a heavy, medium skillet, heat ¼ inch of cooking oil. Fry strips in hot oil, half at a time, about 1 minute or until crisp and light brown. Remove with a slotted spoon; drain on paper towels.

*Note: When seeding and chopping a fresh chile pepper, protect your hands with plastic gloves; the oils in the pepper can irritate your skin. Also, avoid direct contact with your eyes. If you touch the chile pepper, wash your hands thoroughly.

Tantalizing Turkey Chili

MAKES 6 SERVINGS.

David Hannan bases his high-fiber main dish on turkey with black beans and seasons it with the traditional ingredients, such as chili powder, red pepper and cumin. He throws in a little cocoa powder and a splash of coffee for an unexpected, delicious twist.

1	cup chopped onion
¾	cup chopped green sweet pepper
¾	cup chopped red sweet pepper
3	cloves garlic, minced
2	teaspoons olive or canola oil
1	pound uncooked ground turkey or uncooked turkey, chopped
1	28-ounce can crushed tomatoes in puree
1	15-ounce can black beans, rinsed and drained
¼	cup cider vinegar
2	to 3 tablespoons strong brewed coffee
2	to 3 teaspoons chili powder
2	teaspoons unsweetened cocoa powder
1	teaspoon ground cumin
¼	to ½ teaspoon ground red pepper
	Shredded cheddar cheese (optional)
	Finely chopped onion (optional)

1. In a Dutch oven, cook the 1 cup chopped onion, green and red sweet peppers and garlic in hot oil over medium-high heat for 3 minutes. Add turkey. Cook and stir for 3 minutes or until turkey is brown. Drain fat.

2. Add tomatoes, black beans, 1 cup water, vinegar, coffee, chili powder, cocoa powder, cumin and ground red pepper. Bring to boiling; reduce heat. Simmer, covered, for 30 minutes, stirring the mixture occasionally.

3. To serve, ladle chili into soup bowls. Sprinkle with cheddar cheese and additional finely chopped onion, if you like.

Prep: 25 minutes Cook: 30 minutes
Nutrition facts per serving: 243 cal., 8 g fat, 60 mg chol., 561 mg sodium, 25 g carbo., 7 g fiber, 20 g pro.

Winter Beef Stew

MAKES 6 SERVINGS.

Nothing warms the soul on a snowy winter day like a steaming bowl of this all-time favorite classic. This version includes a few surprises. Go ahead, have a seat by the fire and dig in.

1   pound boneless beef chuck, cut into ¾-inch cubes
2   tablespoons cooking oil
2   14-ounce cans beef broth
2   teaspoons Worcestershire sauce
2   teaspoons snipped fresh oregano or ¾ teaspoon dried oregano, crushed
2   teaspoons snipped fresh basil or ¾ teaspoon dried basil, crushed
½   teaspoon black pepper
2   cups cubed Yukon gold potatoes or other potatoes
1   cup frozen cut green beans
1   cup sliced carrots
1   cup sliced celery
1   15½-ounce can Great Northern beans, rinsed and drained
1   14½-ounce can diced tomatoes
1   small yellow summer squash or zucchini, sliced

Prep: 30 minutes Cook: 1 hour 25 minutes
Nutrition facts per serving: 307 cal., 7 g fat, 36 mg chol., 552 mg sodium, 33 g carbo., 6 g fiber, 27 g pro.

1. In a Dutch oven, brown meat, half at a time, in oil. Drain fat. Return meat to pan. Stir in broth, Worcestershire, dried herbs (if using) and pepper; bring to boiling. Reduce heat; simmer, covered, for 1 hour.

2. Stir in potatoes, green beans, carrots and celery. Bring to boiling. Reduce heat; simmer, covered, for 20 minutes. Stir in Great Northern beans, tomatoes, squash and the fresh herbs, if using. Return to boiling; reduce heat. Simmer, covered, for 5 minutes more.

Hearty Pork and Ale Stew

MAKES 6 SERVINGS.

This robust pork stew takes on an autumn orange from the russet-colored sweet potatoes. It celebrates the season with assorted root vegetables, apples and tomatoes simmered with melt-in-your-mouth pork sirloin.

2	tablespoons all-purpose flour
½	teaspoon crushed red pepper
1	pound boneless pork sirloin
2	cloves garlic, minced
1	tablespoon cooking oil
3	cups vegetable broth
1	12-ounce can beer or 1½ cups vegetable broth
2	large sweet potatoes, peeled and cut into 1-inch cubes
3	medium parsnips, peeled and sliced ¾ inch thick
1	medium onion, cut into wedges
2	tablespoons snipped fresh thyme or 1½ teaspoons dried thyme, crushed
1	tablespoon brown sugar
1	tablespoon Dijon-style mustard
4	large plum tomatoes, coarsely chopped
2	small green apples, cored and cut into wedges

Prep: 30 minutes Cook: 35 minutes
Nutrition facts per serving: 288 cal., 7 g fat, 48 mg chol., 571 mg sodium, 36 g carbo., 6 g fiber, 20 g pro.

1. In a plastic bag, combine flour and red pepper. Trim fat from meat. Cut the meat into ¾-inch cubes. Add the meat cubes, a few at a time, to the flour mixture, shaking to coat meat.

2. In a 4-quart Dutch oven, cook meat and garlic in hot oil until the meat is brown. Stir in the vegetable broth, beer, sweet potatoes, parsnips, onion, thyme, brown sugar and mustard.

3. Bring to boiling; reduce heat. Simmer, covered, for 30 minutes. Stir in tomatoes and apples. Return to boiling; reduce heat. Simmer, covered, about 5 minutes more or until meat, vegetables and apples are tender.

Beef with Udon Soup

MAKES 6 SERVINGS.

This beef and noodle soup lets Executive Chef Takashi Yagihashi of Tribute restaurant in Farmington Hills, Michigan, share his Japanese heritage with his children. The test kitchen added some options to substitute when you can't find an ingredient.

6½ cups beef broth
2 tablespoons tamari shoyu (dark Japanese soy sauce) or soy sauce
2 tablespoons shoyu (light Japanese soy sauce) or soy sauce
1 tablespoon sugar
3 quarts cold water
12 ounces packaged dried udon (broad, Japanese wheat noodles) or 12 ounces dried fettuccine
8 ounces boneless beef sirloin steak, very thinly sliced across the grain into bite-size strips
1 cup firmly packed, small fresh spinach leaves
4 green onions, thinly sliced (½ cup)
Ground red pepper (optional)

Start to Finish: 30 minutes
Nutrition facts per serving: 280 cal., 2 g fat, 18 mg chol., 1,512 mg sodium, 45 g carbo., 2 g fiber, 20 g pro.

1. For the soup broth: In a large saucepan, combine the broth, dark soy sauce, light soy sauce and sugar. Bring to boiling; reduce heat. Set aside; keep warm.

2. For the noodles: In a Dutch oven or large pot, bring water to boiling. Add the udon or dried fettuccine, a little at a time, so the water does not stop boiling. Cook according to package directions until noodles are just tender; drain. Transfer noodles to 4 to 6 soup bowls.

3. Return the soup broth to boiling. Add the beef and spinach. Cook, covered, for 2 to 3 minutes or until beef reaches desired doneness. Ladle the hot soup mixture over the noodles in the soup bowls. Top with green onions. Sprinkle with red pepper, if you like.

Big Sky Beef and Mushrooms

MAKES 4 SERVINGS.

This flavor-packed beef dish is perfect company fare because you can make the sauce ahead. Don't be intimidated by the amount of garlic; as it cooks it takes on a wonderfully mellow, nutty flavor.

1 pound beef tenderloin steak or sirloin steak

3 dried ancho or pasilla chile peppers

1 14-ounce can beef broth (1¾ cups)

1 large onion, coarsely chopped

¼ cup coarsely chopped dried tomatoes (not oil-packed)

¼ cup minced garlic (24 cloves)

3 tablespoons tomato paste

2 tablespoons red wine vinegar

1 tablespoon dried oregano, crushed

1 tablespoon brown sugar

1 bay leaf

2 tablespoons unsalted butter or olive oil

3 cups halved fresh brown mushrooms

2 cups hot cooked rice or noodles

Freeze: 30 minutes Prep: 10 minutes
Cook: 28 minutes Cool: 15 minutes
Nutrition facts per serving: 389 cal.,
16 g fat, 86 mg chol., 236 mg sodium,
32 g carbo., 3 g fiber, 30 g pro.

1. Partially freeze beef. Thinly slice across the grain into bite-size strips. Set aside.

2. For sauce: Remove stem and seeds from ancho or pasilla chiles. Heat a heavy medium skillet over medium-low heat. Add chiles and cook for 2 to 4 minutes or until fragrant and pliable, turning occasionally. Remove from skillet.

3. In a large saucepan, combine the chiles, beef broth, onion, dried tomatoes, garlic, tomato paste, vinegar, oregano, brown sugar and bay leaf. Bring to boiling; reduce heat. Simmer, uncovered, for 20 minutes, stirring occasionally. Cool slightly. Remove bay leaf and discard.

4. In a food processor bowl or blender container, process or blend sauce, half at a time, until almost smooth. Set aside*.

5. In a large skillet, cook and stir half of the meat in hot butter or olive oil over medium-high heat for 3 minutes. Remove meat from skillet. Add remaining meat and mushrooms. Cook and stir for 3 minutes. Return all meat to skillet. Add enough sauce (about ¾ cup) to coat the mixture. Cook and stir over medium heat until heated through. Serve with rice or noodles. Pass remaining sauce.

Note: At this point you can cool the sauce and store it in a covered container in the refrigerator for up to a week or in the freezer for up to 3 months.

Souper Spaghetti

Try this tasty recipe for a quick Sunday night supper. If you like, substitute 4 cups peeled, coarsely chopped fresh tomatoes for the canned tomatoes. Increase the cooking time (about 15 minutes, covered) to cook tomatoes down before adding spaghetti.

1	pound lean ground beef
½	cup chopped onion
1	small green sweet pepper, chopped
½	cup chopped celery (1 stalk)
1	medium carrot, chopped
2	cloves garlic, minced
2½	cups water
2	14½-ounce cans diced tomatoes
1	13- to 15-ounce jar spaghetti sauce
1	tablespoon sugar
½	teaspoon dried Italian seasoning, crushed
½	teaspoon salt
¼	teaspoon black pepper
	Dash crushed red pepper
2	ounces spaghetti, broken into 2-inch pieces
	Fresh herb sprigs (optional)

Start to Finish: 45 minutes
Nutrition facts per serving: 263 cal., 9 g fat, 48 mg chol., 960 mg sodium, 28 g carbo., 5 g fiber, 17 g pro.

1. In large saucepan or Dutch oven, cook ground beef, onion, sweet pepper, celery, carrot and garlic over medium heat until vegetables are tender and meat is brown. Drain excess fat.

2. Add water, undrained tomatoes, spaghetti sauce, sugar, Italian seasoning, salt, black pepper and red pepper. Bring mixture to boiling. Add broken spaghetti. Return to boiling; reduce heat. Boil gently, uncovered, for 12 to 15 minutes or until spaghetti is tender. Serve immediately. Garnish with herb sprigs, if you like.

Roasted Poblano Chile and Beef Stroganoff

MAKES 4 SERVINGS.

Beef Stroganoff—that company-special favorite for the mid-20th-century cook—gets a lively global update with poblano chiles, cilantro, and lime to stir things up a bit. Try this spirited one-dish entrée for an intimate dinner party of four.

2	fresh poblano chile peppers
	Cooking oil
2	tablespoons cooking oil
1	pound beef tenderloin steaks or beef tenderloin tips, cut into ½-inch pieces
½	teaspoon salt
2	tablespoons butter
1	cup finely chopped onion
2	cups sliced fresh crimini mushrooms (6 ounces)
1	teaspoon all-purpose flour
⅔	cup chicken broth
½	cup whipping cream
1½	teaspoons Dijon-style mustard
6	ounces dried egg noodles
¼	cup dairy sour cream
2	tablespoons snipped fresh cilantro
1	tablespoon lime juice
	Salt and black pepper
	Snipped fresh cilantro (optional)

Prep: 20 minutes Roast: 15 minutes
Stand: 20 minutes Cook: 20 minutes Oven: 425°F
Nutrition facts per serving: 634 cal.,
39 g fat, 160 mg chol., 608 mg sodium,
39 g carbo., 2 g fiber, 34 g pro.

1. For roasted poblano peppers: Quarter the chiles; remove the seeds and membranes *. Place chile quarters, cut sides down, on a foil-lined baking sheet. Lightly brush skins with oil. Bake, uncovered, in a 425° oven for 15 to 20 minutes or until the skins are charred and blistered. Wrap chiles in the foil and let stand for 20 minutes or until cool enough to handle. Using a sharp knife, gently and slowly remove blistered skin in strips from chiles; discard skin. Coarsely chop chiles. Set aside.

2. In a large skillet (preferably cast iron), heat the 2 tablespoons oil over medium-high heat. Add half of the meat and ¼ teaspoon of the salt. Cook and stir over medium-high heat for 2 to 3 minutes or to desired doneness. Remove from skillet. Repeat with remaining meat and salt. Remove meat from skillet. Wipe out skillet with paper towels.

3. For sauce: In same skillet, heat the 2 tablespoons butter over medium heat. Add onion and mushrooms; cook and stir for 8 to 10 minutes or until tender and golden. Sprinkle flour over onion and mushroom mixture. Cook and stir for 1 minute.

4. Add the chopped chiles, chicken broth, whipping cream and mustard. Cook, stirring constantly, over medium heat for 5 to 7 minutes or until mixture thickens slightly. Remove from heat; cool slightly. Transfer sauce to a food processor bowl or blender container. Cover and process or blend sauce until pureed.

5. Meanwhile, cook egg noodles according to package directions; drain. Set aside.

6. Return sauce to same skillet. Gently whisk in sour cream until well combined. Return meat to skillet. Stir in 2 tablespoons cilantro and lime juice. Season to taste with salt and pepper. Cook and stir for 2 to 3 minutes or until heated through (do not boil). Serve over noodles. Garnish with additional cilantro, if you like.

*Note: See note on handling chile peppers, page 102.

Curried Chicken in Coconut Sauce

MAKES 6 SERVINGS.

This one-bowl wonder relies on several ingredients that add so many layers of flavor to Indian cooking: Spiciness from ginger and curry; the deep, warming flavors of garam masala and the nutty sweetness of coconut milk. It's comfort food—Indian style.

6	skinless, boneless chicken thighs or 6 medium skinless, boneless chicken breast halves (about 1½ pounds total)
2	tablespoons olive oil
1	tablespoon curry powder
¼	teaspoon garam masala or ⅛ teaspoon ground cloves
1	medium onion, chopped
1½	teaspoons grated fresh ginger
1	clove garlic, minced
½	cup chicken broth
½	cup whipping cream
¼	cup unsweetened coconut milk
¾	cup canned undrained diced tomatoes
2	tablespoons unsweetened coconut milk
1	tablespoon cornstarch
1	cup frozen peas
3	cups hot cooked rice
1	tablespoon unsweetened coconut milk

Start to Finish: 35 minutes
Nutrition facts per serving: 420 cal., 20 g fat, 121 mg chol., 250 mg sodium, 31 g carbo., 2 g fiber, 27 g pro.

1. Trim fat from chicken. In a Dutch oven or 12-inch skillet, heat oil over medium-high heat. Add chicken thighs or breast halves. Cook chicken in hot oil over medium-high heat for 2 to 3 minutes or until chicken is lightly browned, turning once. Remove chicken from skillet; set aside, reserving pan drippings.

2. For coconut sauce: In same skillet, stir curry powder and garam masala into the reserved pan drippings. Cook and stir for 1 minute. Add onion, ginger and garlic. Cook and stir until onion is tender but not brown. Add chicken broth, whipping cream and the ¼ cup coconut milk. Bring to boiling; reduce heat. Stir in undrained tomatoes. Simmer, uncovered, for 3 minutes. In a small bowl, stir together the 2 tablespoons coconut milk and cornstarch. Stir cornstarch mixture into curry mixture. Cook and stir over medium heat until thickened and bubbly. Cook and stir for 2 minutes more.

3. Return chicken to the coconut sauce and coat with sauce. Return to boiling; reduce heat. Simmer, covered, for 5 to 6 minutes or until chicken is tender and no longer pink (an instant-read thermometer inserted in chicken registers 180° for thighs or 170° for breasts), turning once. Sprinkle peas over chicken. Remove from heat. Cover and let stand for 5 minutes.

4. Meanwhile, combine hot cooked rice with 1 tablespoon coconut milk. Serve chicken and sauce with coconut-flavored rice.

Chicken Dinner in a Packet

MAKES 4 SERVINGS.

Chicken and vegetables steam in tidy foil packages in your oven. Rennee Schwartz, a yoga instructor and personal trainer in Davenport, Iowa, likes to try different vegetables with the chicken. "People love this dish!" she says. "It's so easy and so tasty."

4	medium skinless, boneless chicken breast halves (1 pound total)
2	tablespoons olive or canola oil
2	tablespoons lemon juice
4	teaspoons snipped fresh basil or 1 teaspoon dried basil or Italian seasoning, crushed
¼	teaspoon salt
¼	teaspoon black pepper
2	cups sliced fresh mushrooms
1	medium zucchini, cut into thin strips (about 1½ cups)
2	medium carrots, cut into thin strips (about ⅔ cup)
	Hot cooked rice or orzo (optional)
	Fresh basil sprigs (optional)

Prep: 25 minutes Bake: 30 minutes Oven: 375°F
Nutrition facts per serving: 222 cal., 9 g fat, 66 mg chol., 221 mg sodium, 6 g carbo., 2 g fiber, 29 g pro.

1. Fold four 28×12-inch pieces of foil in half to make four 14×12-inch rectangles. To assemble chicken bundles, place 1 chicken breast half on each piece of foil, tucking under thin tip of the chicken breast. Fold up edges of foil slightly.

2. In a small bowl, stir together the oil, lemon juice, basil, salt and pepper. Drizzle oil mixture over the chicken breasts. Top with mushrooms, zucchini and carrots, dividing equally among chicken bundles.

3. Bring up 2 opposite edges of foil; seal with a double fold. Fold remaining ends to enclose the chicken and vegetables, leaving space for steam to build. Place foil bundles on a shallow baking pan.

4. Bake in a 375° oven for 30 to 35 minutes or until an instant-read thermometer inserted into chicken registers 170° (carefully open foil when you check doneness).

5. Serve in foil packets or transfer chicken and vegetables to serving plates and drizzle with cooking juices. If you like, serve with rice or orzo and garnish with fresh basil sprigs.

Polenta and Chicken

MAKES 4 SERVINGS.

Here's a new approach to bite-size cooked chicken for kids. The husband-wife chef team from Overland Park, Kansas, Debbie Gold and Michael Smith, serve chicken strips over cornmeal polenta with a tomatoey topper to entice their daughters to try new food.

6	tablespoons olive or canola oil
1	small onion, chopped
1	clove garlic, minced
2½	cups water or chicken broth
¾	cup quick-cooking polenta mix
¼	cup grated Parmesan cheese
¼	cup all-purpose flour
1	teaspoon snipped fresh oregano or ¼ teaspoon dried oregano, crushed
¼	teaspoon salt
¼	teaspoon black pepper
12	ounces packaged skinless, boneless chicken breast strips
2	cups chopped, peeled tomatoes (4 medium) or one 14½-ounce can diced tomatoes
1	teaspoon snipped fresh thyme or ¼ teaspoon dried thyme, crushed
¼	teaspoon salt
¼	teaspoon black pepper
	Parmesan cheese (optional)

Start to Finish: 45 minutes
Nutrition facts per serving: 543 cal., 24 g fat, 54 mg chol., 610 mg sodium, 53 g carbo., 7 g fiber, 29 g pro.

1. For polenta: In a medium saucepan, heat 2 tablespoons of the oil over medium-high heat. Add the onion and garlic. Cook and stir until the onion is tender, but not brown. Add water or broth. Bring mixture to boiling. Stir in polenta. Cook and stir over low heat for 5 minutes or until thickened. Stir in ¼ cup Parmesan cheese. Season to taste with salt and pepper. Set aside; keep warm.

2. In a plastic bag, combine flour, oregano, ¼ teaspoon salt and ¼ teaspoon pepper. Add chicken strips, a few at a time, shaking to coat. In a very large nonstick skillet, heat 2 tablespoons of the oil over medium-high heat. Add chicken strips. Cook and stir in hot oil for 2 to 4 minutes or until chicken is no longer pink. Remove chicken strips from skillet; keep warm.

3. For sauce: Thoroughly wipe out the skillet with paper towels. In the same skillet heat the remaining 2 tablespoons oil over medium-high heat. Add the tomatoes, thyme, ¼ teaspoon salt and ¼ teaspoon pepper. Cook and stir over medium heat for 3 to 5 minutes or until sauce is slightly thickened.

4. To serve, pour the warm polenta into a shallow serving bowl. Top with chicken strips. Pour the sauce over chicken. Sprinkle with additional Parmesan cheese, if you like.

Angel Hair Carbonara

MAKES 6 SERVINGS.

Onion and garlic add character to this main-dish pasta; the turkey bacon makes it sublime. It has less fat than the traditional carbonara recipe, but you'll never miss it. Make it a meal with slices of crusty French bread and butter.

6	slices turkey bacon or bacon, sliced crosswise into thin strips
	Olive oil
1	large onion, coarsely chopped (1 cup)
2	cloves garlic, minced
2	tablespoons all-purpose flour
2	cups fat-free half-and-half
1	cup light ricotta cheese
¼	cup snipped fresh parsley
¼	cup finely shredded Parmesan or Romano cheese
¼	teaspoon freshly ground black pepper
12	ounces dried capellini (angel hair pasta)
1	tablespoon finely shredded Parmesan or Romano cheese

Start to Finish: 30 minutes
Nutrition facts per serving: 399 cal., 9 g fat, 25 mg chol., 374 mg sodium, 57 g carbo., 2 g fiber, 17 g pro.

1. In a large nonstick skillet, cook bacon until crisp. Using a slotted spoon, remove bacon from skillet. Drain on paper towels. Set aside. Reserve 1 tablespoon drippings in skillet. (If no drippings, use 1 tablespoon olive oil.)

2. Cook onion and garlic in drippings or oil over medium heat for 5 minutes or until tender. Stir in flour. Stir in half-and-half all at once. Cook and stir over medium heat until slightly thickened and bubbly. Cook and stir for 1 minute more. Stir in the reserved bacon, ricotta cheese, parsley, ¼ cup Parmesan cheese and pepper. Stir until smooth.

3. Meanwhile, cook pasta according to package directions; drain well. Return to hot pan. Immediately pour the sauce mixture over pasta; toss until combined.

4. To serve, transfer pasta to a large serving dish. Sprinkle with the remaining 1 tablespoon Parmesan cheese.

Pizza Quiches

MAKES 12 QUICHES.

This recipe often appears when Loren Smith-Loncaric cooks with her 6-year-old son Calvin. There's pastry to press into muffin cups, cheese to sprinkle and eggs to break. The pastry chef for Sanford's restaurant in Milwaukee knows it's the perfect recipe for Calvin.

½ of a 15-ounce package folded unbaked piecrust (1 crust)

3 ounces cooked ham, salami, pepperoni, summer sausage and/or prosciutto, chopped (about ⅔ cup)

3 ounces cheddar, mozzarella, provolone and/or Swiss cheese, cut into ½-inch cubes

1 tomato, chopped (¾ cup)

2 slightly beaten eggs

⅓ cup milk

1 tablespoon snipped fresh chives, parsley, basil or oregano (optional)

Prep: 15 minutes Bake: 20 minutes
Cool: 5 minutes Oven: 375°F
Nutrition facts per serving: 140 cal., 9 g fat, 51 mg chol., 219 mg sodium, 10 g carbo., 0 g fiber, 5 g pro.

1. For crust: Let piecrust stand at room temperature according to package directions. On a lightly floured surface, roll piecrust dough to a 13-inch circle. Cut dough into twelve 3-inch circles. Lightly grease twelve 2½-inch muffin cups. Place the pastry rounds in the prepared muffin cups, pressing the pastry lightly into muffin cups (pastry will not go all the way up the sides of muffin cups).

2. Divide ham and cheese among the pastry-lined muffin cups. Sprinkle each with some of the tomato. In a small bowl, stir together the eggs and milk. Spoon about 1 tablespoon of the egg mixture into each muffin cup. Sprinkle each with snipped herbs, if you like.

3. Bake in a 375° oven for 20 minutes or until egg mixture is set and tops are golden. Cool quiches in pan for 5 minutes. Remove from cups. Serve warm.

Ham and Cheese Frittata

MAKES 4 SERVINGS.

Unlike a French omelet, which is served with filling inside a cooked and folded egg mixture, all the ingredients of a frittata are mixed with the eggs and not folded at all. A fruit salad makes a perfect accompaniment.

1   cup refrigerated or frozen egg product, thawed, or 1 cup beaten eggs (any combination of whole eggs and egg whites; don't use all egg whites)

¼   cup fat-free milk

¼   cup light dairy sour cream

2   tablespoons grated Parmesan cheese

¼   teaspoon black pepper

½   cup finely chopped onion (1 medium)

⅔   cup chopped reduced-fat and reduced-sodium cooked ham

2   teaspoons olive oil or canola oil

¼   cup shredded part-skim mozzarella cheese (1 ounce)

Chopped tomato (optional)

Snipped fresh chives (optional)

Light dairy sour cream (optional)

Start to Finish: 30 minutes

Nutrition facts per serving: 137 cal., 6 g fat, 22 mg chol., 469 mg sodium, 5 g carbo., 0 g fiber, 15 g pro.

1. In a medium bowl, whisk together egg product or eggs, milk, ¼ cup sour cream, Parmesan cheese and pepper; set aside.

2. In a large nonstick skillet, cook onion and ham in hot oil over medium heat about 5 minutes or until onion is tender. Evenly spread cooked onion and ham mixture in the bottom of skillet.

3. Slowly add egg mixture to the skillet. Cook over medium heat. As the egg mixture sets, run a spatula around the edge of the skillet, lifting egg mixture to allow uncooked portion to flow underneath. Continue cooking and lifting edges until mixture is almost set (surface will be moist).

4. Remove skillet from heat. Sprinkle with the mozzarella cheese. Cover and let stand for 3 to 4 minutes or until top is set. If you like, sprinkle with chopped tomato and chives. Loosen bottom of frittata with a spatula. To serve, cut into wedges and serve with additional sour cream, if you like.

Test Kitchen Tip: Although you can use a regular skillet, a large skillet with flared sides makes the task of cooking a frittata easier.

Chef's Macaroni and Cheese

MAKES 6 SERVINGS.

When Michael Symon cooks with his 15-year-old stepson, Kyle Shanahan, he emphasizes the fun of the experience, not the work. The executive chef of Lola Bistro & Wine Bar in Cleveland, Ohio, gives familiar macaroni and cheese a kid-friendly twist.

2	cups whipping cream
1	tablespoon snipped fresh rosemary
1	teaspoon kosher salt
¼	teaspoon freshly ground black pepper
8	ounces dried rigatoni pasta
1	tablespoon olive oil
12	ounces skinless, boneless chicken breast halves, cut into bite-size pieces
¼	teaspoon paprika
¼	teaspoon kosher salt
⅛	teaspoon freshly ground black pepper
3	ounces soft goat cheese (chèvre), crumbled, or one 3-ounce package cream cheese, cut up and softened
2	plum tomatoes, chopped

Prep: 15 minutes Cook: 30 minutes
Nutrition facts per serving: 544 cal., 36 g fat, 149 mg chol., 518 mg sodium, 32 g carbo., 1 g fiber, 22 g pro.

1. In a large saucepan, combine whipping cream, rosemary, the 1 teaspoon kosher salt and ¼ teaspoon black pepper. Bring to boiling; reduce heat. Boil gently, uncovered, for 25 to 30 minutes or until mixture is reduced to 1⅓ cups, stirring occasionally.

2. Cook pasta according to package directions. Drain; keep warm.

3. In a large skillet, heat the olive oil over medium-high heat. Add chicken. Cook and stir for 2 minutes. Sprinkle with paprika, the ¼ teaspoon kosher salt and the ⅛ teaspoon pepper. Cook and stir for 1 to 2 minutes more or until chicken is no longer pink.

4. Stir the cooked pasta, chicken, cheese and tomatoes into the whipping cream mixture. Cook and stir for 2 minutes or until heated through. Serve immediately.

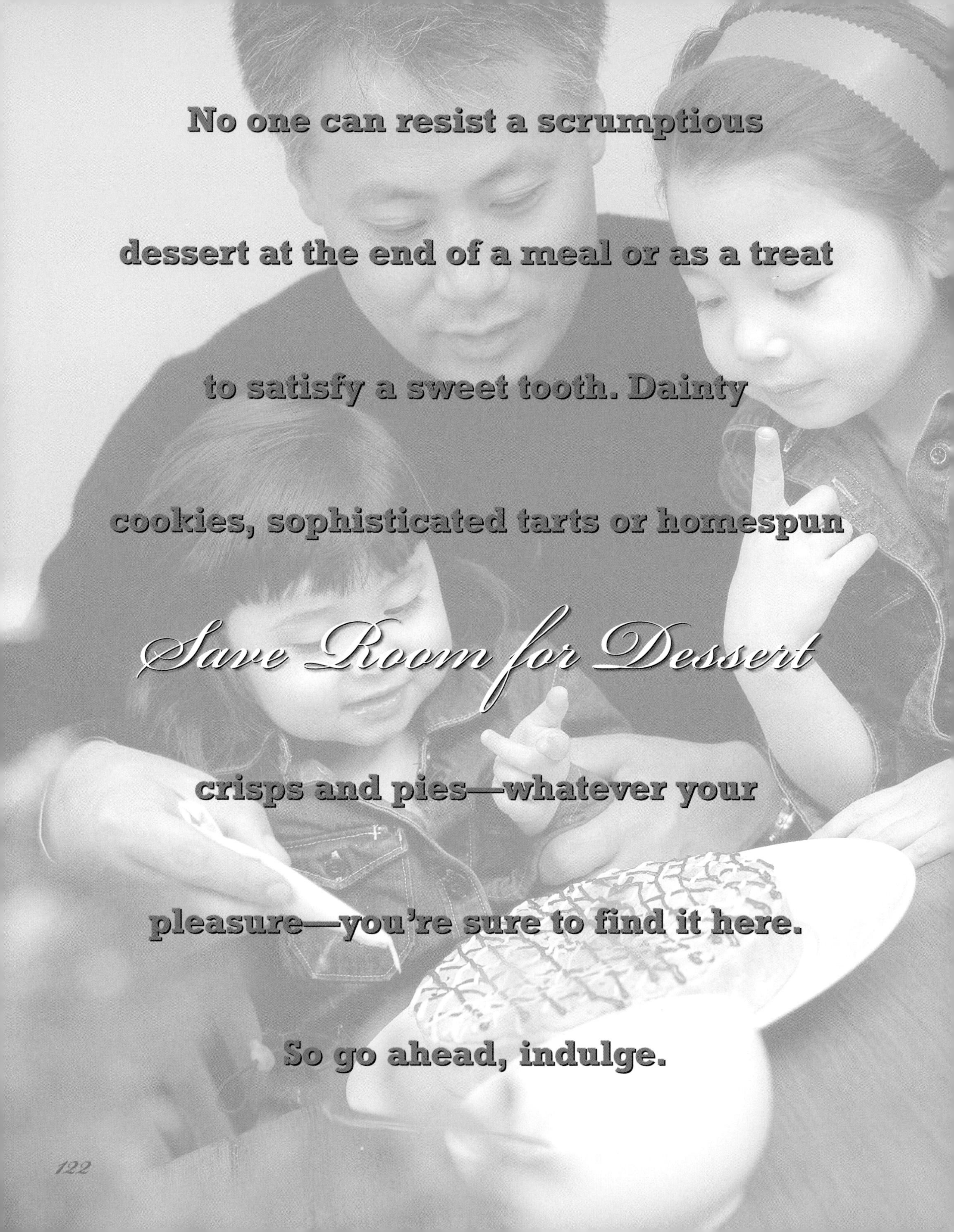

No one can resist a scrumptious

dessert at the end of a meal or as a treat

to satisfy a sweet tooth. Dainty

cookies, sophisticated tarts or homespun

Save Room for Dessert

crisps and pies—whatever your

pleasure—you're sure to find it here.

So go ahead, indulge.

End-of-the-Season Cherry-Lemon Pie, page 142

Chocolate Crème Brûlée Napoleon

MAKES 8 SERVINGS.

Layered dark chocolate custard and buttery phyllo make this version of a Napoleon extra decadent. Top with any berries you have on hand. Try a combination of strawberries and raspberries.

3 cups whipping cream
6 ounces bittersweet or semisweet chocolate, chopped
9 beaten egg yolks
¾ cup granulated sugar
⅛ teaspoon salt
4 sheets frozen phyllo dough (18x14 inches), thawed
½ cup butter, melted
¼ cup granulated sugar
Bittersweet Chocolate Sauce
2 cups large strawberries, halved lengthwise
Sifted powdered sugar

Prep: 30 minutes Bake: 35 minutes/8 minutes
Chill: Up to 24 hours Oven: 325°/375°F
Nutrition facts per serving: 830 cal., 66 g fat, 406 mg chol., 197 mg sodium, 62 g carbo., 4 g fiber, 9 g pro.

1. For custard: In a heavy saucepan, heat cream until it almost boils; keep warm. In another saucepan, heat chocolate over low heat until melted, stirring constantly. In a large mixing bowl, gradually stir hot chocolate into beaten egg yolks. Add the ¾ cup sugar and salt. Beat with a wire whisk until just combined. Slowly whisk in hot cream.

2. Pour custard mixture into a 3-quart rectangular baking dish. Set baking dish in a large roasting pan on an oven rack. Pour enough hot water into the roasting pan around baking dish to reach halfway up the sides of the baking dish.

3. Bake custard in a 325° oven for 35 to 40 minutes or until a knife inserted near center comes out clean. Remove custard from water bath; cool on a wire rack. Cover with plastic wrap; refrigerate until serving or up to 24 hours. Cut into 16 rectangles.

4. For phyllo: On a cutting board, place 1 sheet of phyllo dough. (Cover the remaining stack of phyllo with plastic wrap; remove sheets one at a time as needed.) Lightly brush phyllo with some of the melted butter, brushing butter all the way to edges. Sprinkle with some of the ¼ cup sugar. Repeat with remaining phyllo, butter and sugar, stacking phyllo sheets on top of one another. Cut phyllo stack into 24 rectangles. Place rectangles on a large foil-lined baking sheet. Bake in a 375° oven about 8 minutes or until golden and crisp. Cool on a wire rack. Set aside.

5. To serve, drizzle some of the Bittersweet Chocolate Sauce on a dessert plate. Place 1 phyllo rectangle in center of plate; top with 1 piece of custard. Place another rectangle on top of custard; top with another piece of custard. Top with a third phyllo rectangle. Drizzle with more sauce; decorate with strawberries. Repeat with remaining sauce, phyllo, custard and strawberries. Sprinkle with powdered sugar. Serve immediately.

Bittersweet Chocolate Sauce: In a heavy small saucepan, heat and stir ⅔ cup whipping cream, 4 ounces chopped bittersweet or semisweet chocolate and ¼ cup sugar over medium-low heat until chocolate is melted. Cover; cool to room temperature.

Banana Pierogies

MAKES 6 PIEROGIES.

Michael Symon, executive chef of Lola Bistro & Wine Bar in Cleveland, Ohio, fills this Polish dumpling with a sweet banana mixture. He finishes it off in a way that kids of all ages love—with chocolate sauce, ice cream and bananas or strawberries.

2	tablespoons butter
2	tablespoons brown sugar
2	ripe medium bananas, chopped (1 cup)
¼	teaspoon ground cinnamon
¼	teaspoon ground nutmeg
1¾	cups all-purpose flour
2	tablespoons sifted powdered sugar
¾	teaspoon ground cinnamon
¼	cup butter, softened
½	cup dairy sour cream
1	egg
3	quarts cold water
¼	cup cooking oil
2	tablespoons butter
	Chocolate or caramel ice cream topping
	Vanilla ice cream or your favorite flavor ice cream
	Sliced bananas and/or strawberries (optional)

Prep: 45 minutes Chill: 30 minutes
Cook: 3 minutes/batch

Nutrition facts per pierogie: 622 cal., 37 g fat, 133 mg chol., 257 mg sodium, 68 g carbo., 2 g fiber, 9 g pro.

1. For filling: In a medium skillet, melt 2 tablespoons butter over medium heat. Stir in the brown sugar until melted. Add the chopped bananas. Cook and gently stir over medium heat for 2 minutes or until bananas are soft; sprinkle with ¼ teaspoon cinnamon and nutmeg. Remove from heat; mash mixture. Cover and chill for at least 30 minutes.

2. For dough: In a small bowl, combine flour, powdered sugar and ¾ teaspoon cinnamon. In a large mixing bowl, beat the ¼ cup butter with an electric mixer on medium speed for 30 seconds. Add sour cream and egg; beat until well combined. Stir in the flour mixture until combined and all the dough is moistened.

3. On a lightly floured surface, gently knead dough 12 to 15 strokes or until dough holds together. Roll the dough to about ⅛-inch thick. Cut into six 5-inch circles.

4. Place about 2 tablespoons of the banana filling in the center of each dough round. Lightly moisten the edge of each dough round with water. Gently fold 1 side of the dough over filling to make a semicircle. Using the floured tines of a fork, press edges together to seal.

5. In a Dutch oven or large pot, bring water to boiling. Stir in oil. Add pierogies 3 at a time (do not crowd so the water doesn't stop boiling). Cook pierogies about 2 minutes or until they float. Immediately remove, using a slotted spoon; drain.

6. In a very large skillet, melt the remaining 2 tablespoons butter over medium heat. Add the pierogies, making sure they don't touch each other. Cook in hot butter for 1 to 2 minutes on each side or until pierogies are golden brown.

7. To serve, drizzle dessert plates with chocolate or caramel ice cream topping. Place warm pierogies on plates. Top with ice cream and add sliced bananas and/or strawberries, if you like.

Apple Charlotte

MAKES 12 SERVINGS.

It's homey, elegant and delicious. That's probably why this baked apple dessert ranks as one of the most popular specialties at the Signature Room in Chicago. Don't let the beautiful presentation deter you; it's easy to make.

12 medium Granny Smith apples (about 4 pounds)
¼ cup butter
½ cup sifted powdered sugar
1 tablespoon ground cinnamon
2 teaspoons finely shredded lemon peel
½ cup coarsely chopped dried tart cherries or cranberries
½ cup chopped walnuts
Butter and sifted powdered sugar
18 thin slices firm-textured white bread (1 pound)
½ cup butter, melted
Sifted powdered sugar
2 apples, halved and/or sliced (optional)
Scented geranium leaves (optional)
Vanilla ice cream (optional)

Prep: 30 minutes Cook: 15 minutes
Bake: 20 minutes Cool: 30 minutes Oven: 425°F
Nutrition facts per serving: 347 cal.,
18 g fat, 33 mg chol., 327 mg sodium,
46 g carbo., 4 g fiber, 4 g pro.

1. For filling: Peel, core and thinly slice the apples (should have about 12 cups); set aside. In a very large skillet, melt the ¼ cup butter over medium heat. Stir in the ½ cup powdered sugar, cinnamon and lemon peel. Add the apple slices and cherries, stirring to coat. Cook apple mixture, uncovered, over medium heat for 15 to 20 minutes or until apples are tender and mixture is very thick, stirring occasionally (apple mixture must be thick or it will make bread soggy). Stir in nuts; set aside.

2. For charlotte: Lightly butter a 2-quart soufflé dish or casserole. Lightly dust with powdered sugar; set aside.

3. Trim crusts from the bread; discard crusts and end pieces (or save for another use). Halve bread slices diagonally to make triangles. Generously brush the bread triangles on both sides with melted butter. Line the bottom of prepared dish with some of the bread triangles by fitting the pieces close together and overlapping slightly (about ¼ inch), carefully arranging and trimming as needed (reserve trimmings). Completely line the side of the soufflé dish or casserole with some of the remaining bread triangles, overlapping as necessary. Fit reserved trimmings into open spaces.

4. Fill the prepared bread-lined dish with the apple filling. Completely cover apple filling with the remaining bread triangles, overlapping and fitting reserved trimmings into any open spaces.

5. Bake, uncovered, in a 425° oven for 20 to 25 minutes or until heated through and golden brown. Remove from oven; cool about 30 minutes. Loosen sides and invert onto a large serving dish. (Be sure the serving dish has a slight lip to catch any juice and/or filling. Don't unmold the charlotte until it's ready to serve).

6. Just before serving, dust with additional powdered sugar. Garnish with apple pieces and scented geranium leaves and serve with ice cream, if you like.

Spiced Pumpkin Bread Pudding

MAKES 8 SERVINGS.

At the Top of the Rock Restaurant near Branson, Missouri, chefs mix spiced pumpkin into their bread pudding for a new version of this age-old comfort food. If you don't have pumpkin seeds on hand, sprinkle toasted pecans or walnuts on top.

1	15-ounce can pumpkin
¾	cup sugar
2	teaspoons pumpkin pie spice
3	eggs
1	cup milk
¼	cup whipping cream, half-and-half or light cream
1	tablespoon brandy (optional)
1	teaspoon vanilla
5	cups dry French bread cubes
	Whipped cream
	Ground cinnamon
	Toasted pumpkin seeds (optional)

Prep: 15 minutes Bake: 45 minutes
Cool: 30 minutes Oven: 325°F
Nutrition facts per serving: 270 cal.,
12 g fat, 113 mg chol., 168 mg sodium,
36 g carbo., 2 g fiber, 6 g pro.

1. In a large mixing bowl, combine pumpkin, sugar and pumpkin pie spice. Add eggs. Beat lightly with a rotary beater or fork until just combined. Gradually stir in milk, whipping cream, brandy (if you like) and vanilla; mix well. Stir in bread cubes until coated with pumpkin mixture. Pour mixture into an ungreased 2-quart square baking dish.

2. Bake, uncovered, in a 325° oven for 45 minutes. Cool slightly.

3. Serve warm bread pudding on dessert plates and top with whipped cream. Lightly sprinkle with cinnamon and top with a few pumpkin seeds, if you like.

Garden Party Cream Puffs

MAKES 30 CREAM PUFFS.

A hint of grated orange peel in the cocoa whipped cream filling adds something special to these float-off-the-plate party pleasers. These are perfect bite-size treats for any occasion; your guests won't be disappointed.

1 cup water
½ cup unsalted butter
¼ teaspoon salt
1 cup all-purpose flour
4 large eggs
Cocoa Whipped Cream
Chocolate Glaze

Prep: 40 minutes Cool: 10 minutes
Bake: 15 minutes Chill: Up to 2 hours
Oven: 400°F
Nutrition facts per cream puff: 106 cal.,
8 g fat, 48 mg chol., 32 mg sodium,
6 g carbo., 0 g fiber, 2 g pro.

1. Grease 2 large baking sheets. Set aside. In a medium saucepan, combine water, butter and salt. Bring to boiling. Add flour all at once, stirring vigorously. Cook and stir until mixture forms a ball that doesn't separate. Remove from heat. Cool for 10 minutes.

2. Add eggs, one at a time, beating well with a wooden spoon after each. Drop dough by tablespoonfuls into 30 mounds 2 inches apart on prepared baking sheets. For evenly shaped puffs, avoid going back to add more dough to the mounds.

3. Bake in a 400° oven for 15 to 20 minutes or until golden. Remove from baking sheets and cool on wire racks.

4. Cut tops from puffs and remove any soft dough from inside. Fill each with about 1 tablespoon of Cocoa Whipped Cream. Replace cream puff tops. Drizzle Chocolate Glaze over each cream puff. Chill for up to 2 hours or until glaze is set.

Cocoa Whipped Cream: Chill a mixing bowl and beaters of an electric mixer. In bowl, combine 1 cup whipping cream, 3 tablespoons sifted powdered sugar, 1 tablespoon unsweetened cocoa powder and ½ teaspoon vanilla. Add ½ teaspoon finely shredded orange peel, if you like. Beat on low speed until soft peaks form. Makes 2 cups.

Chocolate Glaze: In a small heavy saucepan, combine 4 ounces chopped semisweet chocolate and 2 teaspoons shortening. Cook over low heat until chocolate is melted, stirring frequently. Remove from heat. Stir until smooth.

Crimson Cranberry–Apple Crisp

MAKES 6 SERVINGS.

David Hannan, the fitness and wellness coordinator at Kettering Recreation Center in Ohio, shares this seasonal dessert that pairs sweet apples with tangy cranberries. The delectable recipe includes less sugar and butter than the average fruit crisp.

3	tablespoons granulated sugar
1	teaspoon ground cinnamon
3	cups sliced, peeled cooking apples
2	cups fresh cranberries*
½	cup quick-cooking rolled oats
¼	cup packed brown sugar
2	tablespoons all-purpose flour
¼	teaspoon ground nutmeg or ginger
3	tablespoons butter or margarine
2	tablespoons chopped nuts or coconut (optional)
	Fat-free vanilla ice cream, or frozen yogurt or fat-free half-and-half (optional)

Prep: 15 minutes Bake: 40 minutes
Cool: 30 minutes Oven: 375°F
Nutrition facts per serving without ice cream: 205 cal., 7 g fat, 16 mg chol., 66 mg sodium, 36 g carbo., 4 g fiber, 2 g pro.

1. In a small bowl, combine granulated sugar and cinnamon. Place the apples and cranberries in an ungreased 1½-quart casserole. Sprinkle sugar-cinnamon mixture over fruit. Toss gently to coat. Bake, covered, in a 375° oven for 25 minutes.

2. For topping: In a small mixing bowl, combine the oats, brown sugar, flour and nutmeg. With a pastry blender, cut in butter until mixture resembles coarse crumbs. Stir in nuts or coconut, if you like. Sprinkle topping over the partially cooked fruit mixture.

3. Return to oven and bake, uncovered, for 15 to 20 minutes more or until fruit is tender and topping is golden. Cool slightly. Serve warm with ice cream, frozen yogurt or half-and-half, if you like.

*Note: If you can't find any fresh cranberries, substitute 1 cup dried cranberries.

Blackberry and
Pound Cake Crisp

MAKES 8 SERVINGS.

Here, the fruit crisp, one of summer's favorite (and easiest) desserts, starts with a bonus layer of buttery pound cake. Rich Travis, executive chef of the acclaimed Latitude restaurant in Bay Harbor, Michigan, shares this luscious recipe.

1	10¾-ounce frozen pound cake, thawed
1	cup all-purpose flour
¾	cup packed brown sugar
½	teaspoon ground cinnamon
¼	teaspoon salt
⅓	cup cold butter, cut up
1	cup whipping cream
2	tablespoons all-purpose flour
2	tablespoons granulated sugar
4	cups fresh or frozen blackberries

Prep: 25 minutes Broil: 2 minutes
Bake: 45 minutes Cool: 15 minutes Oven: 350°F
Nutrition facts per serving: 526 cal.,
28 g fat, 105 mg chol., 315 mg sodium,
66 g carbo., 5 g fiber, 5 g pro.

1. Preheat broiler. Cut pound cake into ½-inch slices. Place the slices on a baking sheet. Broil about 4 inches from the heat about 1 minute per side or until slices are lightly toasted. Cut the toasted slices into fourths. Arrange cake pieces in the bottom of a 2-quart rectangular baking dish. Set aside.

2. For topping: In a medium bowl, stir together the 1 cup flour, brown sugar, cinnamon and salt. Using a pastry blender, cut in the butter until the mixture resembles coarse crumbs. Set aside.

3. In a large bowl, whisk together whipping cream, the 2 tablespoons flour and granulated sugar until combined. Fold in fresh or frozen blackberries. Spread the blackberry mixture over pound cake layer. Sprinkle topping over blackberry mixture.

4. Bake in a 350° oven for 45 to 50 minutes or until topping is golden and filling is bubbly. Cool on a wire rack for 15 minutes. Serve warm.

Fun Fruit Tart

MAKES 8 SERVINGS.

When Ken Goff, executive chef at Dakota Restaurant in Saint Paul, makes this tart, his daughter, Cecilia, rolls out the dough and arranges the fruit on top before it's baked. Need to save time? Substitute refrigerated piecrust for the homemade pastry, if you like.

1¼ cups unbleached all-purpose flour or whole wheat pastry flour

¼ teaspoon salt

½ cup cold unsalted butter, cut into small pieces

5 tablespoons ice water

¼ to ½ cup sugar (depending on sweetness of the fruit)

2 tablespoons all-purpose flour

4 cups sliced, peeled and cored pears or apples, or halved and pitted apricots, peeled and sliced peaches or sliced nectarines (about 2 pounds)

1 beaten egg yolk

1 tablespoon half-and-half, light cream or milk

1 cup whipping cream

Prep: 40 minutes Chill: 30 minutes
Bake: 40 minutes Cool: 30 minutes Oven: 375°F
Nutrition facts per serving: 366 cal., 25 g fat, 101 mg chol., 88 mg sodium, 35 g carbo., 3 g fiber, 4 g pro.

1. For pastry: In a medium bowl, combine the 1¼ cups flour and salt. Using a pastry blender, cut butter into flour mixture until mixture resembles coarse crumbs. Make a well in center of mixture. Add ice water all at once. Using a rubber spatula or a fork, stir until dry ingredients are moistened. Shape dough into a ball.

2. Flatten dough into a disk. If necessary, cover dough with plastic wrap and refrigerate for 30 minutes or until easy to handle. Let dough stand for 5 to 10 minutes. Place dough on a lightly floured surface. Sprinkle top of pastry with flour. Roll dough from center to edge to form a 13-inch circle of even thickness. Brush away excess flour from top of dough; fold dough in half and brush away excess flour. Fold dough in half again and brush away flour. Pick up dough; turn over to expose final floured surface and brush away flour. Carefully unfold dough onto a 12-inch pizza pan or very large baking sheet, being careful not to stretch it. (If pastry is soft, set the pizza pan or baking sheet in the refrigerator and chill for 30 minutes.)

3. For filling: In a large bowl, combine the sugar and 2 tablespoons flour. Stir in fruit; gently toss to evenly coat. Mound fruit mixture in center of pastry, leaving a 3-inch border. (Or arrange fruit slices from the center out toward the edges in overlapping rows, leaving a 3-inch border.) Carefully fold the pastry border up and over fruit, pleating pastry as necessary to fit. In a small bowl, combine the egg yolk and half-and-half; brush on top and sides of crust. Bake in a 375° oven for 40 to 45 minutes or until crust is golden. Cool for 30 minutes on pizza pan or baking sheet.

4. Meanwhile, pour whipping cream into a 2- to 3-cup container with a tight-fitting lid. Cover; place in freezer for 20 minutes. Remove from freezer; vigorously shake container for 3 to 4 minutes or until cream is slightly thickened but still pourable. Cut tart into 8 wedges; place in dessert bowls. Pour thickened cream over each wedge.

Chocolate Walnut Tart

MAKES 12 TO 16 SERVINGS.

Kids of all ages will love this chocolaty dessert from Takashi Yagihashi, executive chef for Tribute restaurant in Farmington Hills, Michigan. It's fancy enough to serve company, but enticing enough for small children.

2¼	cups all-purpose flour
¾	cup cold unsalted butter, cut into small pieces
½	teaspoon salt
6	to 8 tablespoons ice water
4	eggs
1¼	cups sugar
3	tablespoons unsalted butter, melted
1	teaspoon vanilla
¾	cup all-purpose flour
1¾	cups coarsely chopped toasted walnuts
1½	cups semisweet chocolate pieces
	Vanilla ice cream (optional)
	Fudge ice cream topping (optional)

Prep: 40 minutes Chill: 1 hour Bake: 51 minutes
Cool: 1½ hours Oven: 450/350°F
Nutrition facts per serving: 427 cal., 26 g fat, 84 mg chol., 93 mg sodium, 45 g carbo., 2 g fiber, 7 g pro.

1. For crust: Place steel blade in food processor bowl. Add the 2¼ cups flour, the ¾ cup butter and salt. Cover; process with on/off turns until most of mixture resembles cornmeal, but with a few larger pieces. With processor running, quickly add 6 tablespoons water through feed tube. Stop processor when all water is added; scrape down sides. Process with two on/off turns (mixture may not all be moistened). Remove dough from bowl; shape into a ball, kneading as necessary. (Or in a medium bowl, combine flour and salt; cut in butter using a pastry blender. Make a well in center; add 6 to 8 tablespoons ice water, 1 tablespoon at a time. Toss mixture with a fork to moisten after each addition. Shape dough into a ball.) Flatten dough into a disk; cover with plastic wrap. Refrigerate for 1 hour or until dough is easy to handle.

2. On a lightly floured surface, roll dough from center to edges to form a 15-inch circle. Fold pastry in quarters; transfer to a 10-inch springform pan or 10-inch round cake pan. Unfold pastry into pan, being careful not to stretch it. Gently press pastry 2 inches up the sides of springform pan or trim pastry even with top of cake pan.

3. Prick bottom and sides of pastry in pan with a fork. Line pastry with a double thickness of regular foil. Bake in a 450° oven for 8 minutes. Remove foil. Bake 4 to 5 minutes more or until set and dry. Set aside. Reduce oven temperature to 350°.

4. For filling: In a large mixing bowl, beat eggs with an electric mixer on high speed about 5 minutes or until thick and light colored. Gradually add the sugar; beat until light and fluffy. Add the 3 tablespoons melted butter and vanilla; mix well. Add the ¾ cup flour; mix just until combined, scraping sides of bowl. Stir in nuts and chocolate.

5. Pour filling into partially baked pastry shell. Bake in a 350° oven for 45 minutes until golden brown. Cool for 1½ hours on wire rack; remove sides of springform pan. (Or turn the tart in cake pan out onto a wire rack; invert onto a cake plate.) Serve with ice cream and fudge topping, if you like. Top of cake will crack when cut.

Softhearted Chocolate Cakes

Makes 8 servings.

A rich, soft center makes these chocolaty cakes even more irresistible at the Inn at Kristofer's in Sister Bay, Wisconsin. Terri Milligan tops them with a custard sauce and raspberry sauce. For simplicity, drizzle with raspberry sauce and sprinkle with fresh berries.

1 cup unsalted butter, cut into pieces
8 ounces bittersweet chocolate, chopped, or 1⅓ cups semisweet chocolate pieces
4 eggs
4 egg yolks
½ cup sugar
½ cup all-purpose flour
1 teaspoon vanilla
⅛ teaspoon salt
 Whipped cream (optional)
 Raspberry Sauce (optional)
 Fresh raspberries (optional)

Prep: 25 minutes Bake: 9 minutes
Cool: 1 hour Oven: 350°F
Nutrition facts per serving: 497 cal., 39 g fat, 278 mg chol., 77 mg sodium, 34 g carbo., 2 g fiber, 7 g pro.

1. Lightly butter eight 8-ounce ramekins or 1-cup soufflé dishes; line bottoms with parchment or waxed paper. Place prepared ramekins on a shallow baking pan or on a large baking sheet. Set aside.

2. In a heavy-bottomed, medium saucepan, melt butter and chocolate over low heat, stirring constantly. Remove from heat; cool slightly. In a large mixing bowl, beat eggs and egg yolks with an electric mixer on high speed for 5 minutes or until thick and lemon-colored. Fold a large spoonful of the beaten eggs into the butter-chocolate mixture. Gently fold until combined. Add butter-chocolate mixture to remaining beaten egg mixture and fold in. After a few folds, sprinkle in sugar, flour, vanilla and salt. Continue to fold until the mixture is combined.

3. Quickly divide batter evenly among prepared ramekins. Bake in a 350° oven for 9 to 11 minutes or until cakes feel firm to the touch on top edges, but still soft in the center when pressed with a fingertip. Remove from oven; set ramekins on a wire rack. Let cakes cool completely in ramekins.

4. Line a baking sheet with parchment or waxed paper. When cakes are cool, use a small metal spatula to loosen edges of cakes from ramekins; unmold onto the prepared baking sheet. The centers of the cakes should be soft. (If not serving immediately, cover with plastic wrap and refrigerate until ready to serve.)

5. To serve, place cakes on a microwave-safe plate. Heat in a microwave oven on 100 percent power (high) for 1½ to 2 minutes or until warm (centers will pop up slightly). Serve with whipped cream; garnish with Raspberry Sauce and fresh berries, if you like.

Raspberry Sauce: Thaw one 10-ounce package frozen red raspberries in syrup. In a blender container or food processor bowl, cover and blend or process the berries in syrup until pureed. Strain through a fine sieve. Cover and refrigerate until ready to serve. Makes ⅔ cup.

Scott's Choice Rum Cake

MAKES 16 SERVINGS.

At Pincushion Mountain B&B in Grand Marais, Minnesota, Mary Beattie dresses up a cake mix with nuts and rum, then drizzles it with a buttery rum sauce. She always sets some of the moist cake aside for her husband, Scott. He loves it.

½ cup chopped nuts
1 package 2-layer size yellow cake mix
4 eggs
½ cup cooking oil
½ cup cold water
½ cup rum
Rum Sauce

Prep: 25 minutes Bake: 55 minutes
Stand: 30 minutes Oven: 350°F
Nutrition facts per serving: 369 cal., 21 g fat, (0 g sat. fat), 70 mg chol., 293 mg sodium, 38 g carbo., 1 g fiber, 4 g pro.

1. Generously grease a 10-inch fluted tube pan (12 cup). Sprinkle with nuts.

2. In a large mixing bowl, beat together the dry cake mix, eggs, cooking oil, cold water and rum with an electric mixer on medium speed for 6 minutes.

3. Pour the batter into the prepared tube pan. Bake in a 350° oven for 55 to 60 minutes or until a toothpick inserted in center comes out clean. Place the pan on a wire rack.

4. Prepare the Rum Sauce. With a long-tined fork, poke holes in the top of cake. Spoon the sauce over warm cake while it's still in the pan. Let stand for 30 minutes. Loosen cake and invert onto plate to cool. Loosely cover until serving time.

Rum Sauce: In a medium saucepan, combine 1 cup sugar, ½ cup butter or margarine, ¼ cup water and ¼ cup rum. Cook and stir until the mixture boils. Reduce the heat. Cook and stir for 2 minutes more.

Best Carrot-Pineapple Cake

MAKES 14 SERVINGS.

Pastry Chef Tom Byers *has seen trends come and go during his eight-year stint with the Country Club of Indianapolis. But this carrot cake traditionally remains one of the club diners' favorites.*

2	cups sifted cake flour
1¾	cups sugar
1	tablespoon ground cinnamon
1	teaspoon baking powder
1	teaspoon baking soda
½	teaspoon salt
½	teaspoon ground allspice
1¼	cups finely shredded carrot
1	8¼-ounce can crushed pineapple (syrup pack)
¾	cup mayonnaise
4	eggs
1	cup chopped walnuts, toasted
	Cream Cheese Frosting

Prep: 25 minutes Bake: 30 minutes
Cool: 1 hour, 10 minutes Oven: 350°F
Nutrition facts per serving: 562 cal., 29 g fat, 104 mg chol., 340 mg sodium, 72 g carbo., 2 g fiber, 6 g pro.

1. Grease and flour two 8×1½-inch or 9×1½-inch round baking pans. Set pans aside.

2. In a large mixing bowl, combine the flour, sugar, cinnamon, baking powder, baking soda, salt and allspice. Add carrot, undrained pineapple, mayonnaise and eggs. Beat with an electric mixer on low speed until moistened. Beat on medium speed for 2 minutes, scraping bowl occasionally. Stir in walnuts.

3. Pour batter into the prepared pans. Bake in a 350° oven for 30 to 35 minutes or until a toothpick inserted near the centers comes out clean. Cool in pans on wire racks for 10 minutes. Loosen sides. Remove cakes from pans. Cool thoroughly on wire racks.

4. To assemble, place 1 cake layer on a serving plate. Spread layer with about ½ cup of the Cream Cheese Frosting. Top with second layer. Spread top and sides with the remaining frosting. Store, covered, in refrigerator.

Cream Cheese Frosting: In a large mixing bowl, beat one 8-ounce package cream cheese, softened; ½ cup unsalted butter, softened, and 2 teaspoons vanilla with an electric mixer on medium speed until light and fluffy. Gradually beat in enough sifted powdered sugar (about 4 cups) to make a frosting of spreading consistency. Makes 3½ cups frosting.

Double Berry Vanilla Cream Pie

MAKES 8 SERVINGS.

A double dose of summer-fresh berries tops a tangy-sweet sour cream pudding filling in a toasted almond crust. It's the perfect warm-weather dessert—it requires less than 30 minutes of prep in the kitchen before you tuck the pie in the refrigerator to chill.

Toasted Almond Crust or
    Pastry for a Single-Crust Pie
    (page 64)
1   4-serving size package vanilla
       pudding mix
1¾   cups milk
½   cup dairy sour cream
1   10-ounce package frozen
       strawberries in syrup,
       thawed
1   tablespoon cornstarch
5   cups fresh strawberries, hulled
1   cup fresh blueberries
     Sweetened whipped cream

Prep: 25 minutes   Bake: 10 minutes
Chill: 3 hours   Oven: 450°F
Nutrition facts per serving: 396 cal.,
20 g fat, 30 mg chol., 198 mg sodium,
50 g carbo., 4 g fiber, 6 g pro.

1. Prepare Toasted Almond Pastry or Pastry for Single-Crust Pie. Slightly flatten dough. Roll dough from center to edges to a 12-inch circle. Wrap pastry around rolling pin and ease it into a 9-inch pie plate, being careful not to stretch pastry. Trim pastry ½ inch beyond edge of pie plate; fold under extra pastry and flute edge. Prick bottom and sides of crust. Bake in a 450° oven for 10 to 12 minutes. Cool.

2. For cream filling: cook vanilla pudding mix according to package directions, except use the 1¾ cups milk for the liquid. Cool pudding for 10 minutes. Fold in the sour cream. Spread into bottom of the cooled piecrust. Cover with plastic wrap; chill for 1 hour or until firm.

3. For glaze: place thawed strawberries in a blender container. Cover and blend until nearly smooth. In a small saucepan, stir blended strawberries into cornstarch. Cook and stir until thickened and bubbly. Cook and stir for 2 minutes more. Remove from heat. Cover surface with plastic wrap. Cool to room temperature.

4. To assemble pie, arrange half of the fresh strawberries, stem ends down, over cream layer in pie crust. Sprinkle with half of the blueberries. Drizzle ⅓ of the glaze over the berries. Repeat with remaining berries. Drizzle remaining glaze over berries. Chill for 2 to 4 hours. Serve immediately with whipped cream.

Toasted Almond Crust: In a medium bowl, combine 1¼ cups all-purpose flour, 1 tablespoon sugar and ¼ teaspoon salt. Cut in ⅓ cup shortening until pieces are the size of small peas. Stir in ¼ cup finely chopped toasted almonds. Sprinkle 1 tablespoon water over part of the mixture; gently toss with a fork. Push to side of bowl. Repeat using 1 tablespoon cold water at a time (2 to 3 tablespoons total) until all of the dough is moistened. Form dough into a ball.

Overlook Coconut Cream Pie

MAKES 8 SERVINGS.

It's best to leave room for pie at the Overlook Restaurant near Leavenworth, Indiana. Who can resist a slice of this tantalizing meringue-topped specialty? When you make it at home, if it doesn't disappear in one day, cover and refrigerate it for longer storage.

6	eggs
	Pastry for Single-Crust Pie (page 64)
1	cup sugar
3	tablespoons cornstarch
¼	teaspoon salt
2½	cups milk
3	tablespoons butter
2	teaspoons vanilla
1	cup flaked coconut
½	teaspoon cream of tartar
½	cup sugar
	Shaved coconut or ⅓ cup flaked coconut

Prep: 45 minutes Bake: 13 minutes/25 minutes
Cool: 1 hour Chill: 3 hours Oven: 450°/325°F
Nutrition facts per serving: 533 cal.,
26 g fat, 194 mg chol., 309 mg sodium,
63 g carbo., 1 g fiber, 12 g pro.

1. Separate egg yolks from whites; set aside 4 of the egg whites for meringue. Let stand at room temperature for 30 minutes. (Refrigerate remaining egg whites in a tightly covered container for up to 4 days.) Place yolks in a small bowl; set aside.

2. Prepare Pastry for Single-Crust Pie. On a floured surface, slightly flatten dough. Roll dough from center to edges to a 12-inch circle. Wrap pastry around rolling pin and ease it into a 9-inch pie plate, being careful not to stretch pastry. Trim pastry to ½ inch beyond edge of pie plate. Fold under extra pastry; crimp edge. Prick bottom and sides of pastry with a fork; line with a double thickness of foil. Bake in a 450° oven for 8 minutes. Remove foil. Bake for 5 to 6 minutes more or until golden. Cool.

3. For filling: In a large saucepan, combine the 1 cup sugar, cornstarch and salt. Gradually stir in milk. Cook and stir over medium-high heat until thickened and bubbly. Cook and stir for 2 minutes more. Remove from heat. Slightly beat egg yolks with a rotary beater or fork. Gradually stir about 1 cup of the hot milk mixture into yolks. Pour egg yolk mixture into hot milk mixture in saucepan; stir to combine. Return saucepan to heat. Bring to a gentle boil. Cook and stir for 2 minutes more. Remove from heat. Stir in butter and 1 teaspoon of the vanilla. Stir in the 1 cup coconut; set aside.

4. For meringue: In a large mixing bowl, combine the reserved 4 egg whites, the remaining vanilla and the cream of tartar. Beat with an electric mixer on medium speed about 1 minute or until soft peaks form (tips curl). Gradually add the ½ cup sugar, 1 tablespoon at a time, beating on high speed about 4 minutes more or until mixture forms stiff, glossy peaks (tips stand straight) and sugar dissolves. Pour hot pie filling into baked pastry shell. Immediately spread meringue over hot filling, carefully sealing to edge of pastry to prevent shrinkage. Sprinkle with shaved coconut.

5. Bake in a 325° oven for 25 to 30 minutes or until meringue is lightly browned. Cool on a wire rack for 1 hour. Refrigerate for 3 to 6 hours before serving.

End-of-the-Season
Cherry-Lemon Pie

MAKES 8 SERVINGS.

This cherry pie recipe is too good to pass up. It's from Tim Tiemeyer's mother, Minnie, who lives in Vallonia, a beautiful valley in south-central Indiana. She adds lemon peel to the filling for a citrus accent. If you're a fancy pie maker, add a lattice top.

1¼   cups sugar
3   tablespoons quick-cooking
     tapioca
1   teaspoon finely shredded
     lemon peel
5   cups fresh or frozen
     unsweetened pitted tart
     red cherries
     Pastry for Double-Crust Pie
1   slightly beaten egg white
1   tablespoon water
2   tablespoons butter, cut up
     Coarse sugar (optional)
     Vanilla ice cream (optional)

Prep: 1 hour Bake: 55 minutes Oven: 375°F
Nutrition facts per serving: 478 cal.,
20 g fat, 8 mg chol., 258 mg sodium,
71 g carbo., 3 g fiber, 5 g pro.

1. In a large bowl, stir together the sugar, tapioca and lemon peel. Add cherries; gently toss until coated. Let mixture stand about 15 minutes or until a syrup forms, stirring occasionally. (If using frozen cherries, let mixture stand about 45 minutes or until fruit is partially thawed but still icy.)

2. Meanwhile, prepare Pastry for Double-Crust Pie. On a lightly floured surface, flatten one of the dough balls. Roll dough from center to edges into a 12-inch circle. Wrap pastry circle around a rolling pin; unroll into a 9-inch pie plate.

3. In a small bowl, stir together egg white and water; brush some of the egg white mixture onto pastry in pie plate. Stir cherry mixture; spoon into pastry-lined pie plate. Dot with butter. Trim pastry to edge of pie plate. Roll remaining dough to a 12-inch circle; cut slits in pastry. Place pastry over filling; trim ½ inch beyond edge of pie plate. Fold top pastry under bottom pastry. Crimp edge. Brush with additional egg white mixture; sprinkle with coarse sugar, if you like. Place pie on a baking sheet.

4. To prevent overbrowning, cover edge of pie with a metal piecrust shield or foil. Bake in a 375° oven for 30 minutes (50 minutes for frozen fruit). Remove shield or foil. Bake for 25 to 35 minutes more or until center is bubbly and pastry is golden. Cool on a wire rack. If you like, serve with ice cream.

Pastry for Double-Crust Pie: In a large bowl, stir together 2¼ cups all-purpose flour and ¾ teaspoon salt. Using a pastry blender, cut in ⅔ cup shortening until pieces are pea-size. Sprinkle 1 tablespoon of cold water over part of mixture; gently toss with a fork. Push moistened dough to side of bowl. Repeat, using 1 tablespoon cold water at a time (8 to 10 tablespoons total), until all of the dough is moistened. Shape dough into a ball. Divide dough in half; form each half into a ball.

Note: For a decorative finish, cut pastry dough scraps into desired cutouts. Bake in a 375° oven for 5 to 8 minutes or until golden brown. Use to decorate top of baked pie.

Chocolate Truffle Cookies

Makes about 40 cookies.

If you crave fudgy, rich chocolate, you'll love these cookies from Pincushion Mountain B&B near Grand Marais, Minnesota. Unsweetened and semisweet chocolates blend with cocoa powder in this energy boost.

4	ounces unsweetened chocolate
6	tablespoons butter
2	cups semisweet chocolate pieces (12 ounces)
½	cup all-purpose flour
2	tablespoons unsweetened cocoa powder
¼	teaspoon baking powder
¼	teaspoon salt
1	cup sugar
3	eggs
1½	teaspoons vanilla
1	cup broken pecans or walnuts (optional)

Prep: 25 minutes Chill: 1 hour
Bake: 10 minutes/batch Oven: 350°F
Nutrition facts per cookie: 104 cal., 6 g fat,
21 mg chol., 42 mg sodium, 12 g carbo.,
1 g fiber, 1 g pro.

1. In a small heavy saucepan, melt the unsweetened chocolate, the butter and 1 cup of semisweet chocolate over low heat, stirring constantly. Remove from heat and cool to room temperature.

2. In a small bowl, stir together flour, cocoa powder, baking powder and salt. Set aside.

3. In a large mixing bowl, beat the sugar, eggs and vanilla with an electric mixer for 2 minutes.

4. Beat in the cooled chocolate mixture. Beat in the flour mixture until combined. Stir in the remaining semisweet chocolate pieces and nuts, if you like. Cover and chill dough for at least 1 hour (dough will become stiff after chilling).

5. Drop dough by rounded teaspoons 2 inches apart on a greased cookie sheet.

6. Bake in a 350° oven for 10 minutes or until the edges are firm. Remove to a wire rack to cool.

Mocha-Latte Brownies

MAKES 36 BROWNIES.

A cup of java gives these buttermilk brownies a mild coffee flavor. They get rave reviews from lunch guests who have learned to always save room for Corrine Prins' dessert at Prairie Sky Guest Ranch near Veblen, South Dakota.

2 cups all-purpose flour
2 cups sugar
1 cup strong brewed coffee
½ cup butter or margarine
½ cup shortening
¼ cup unsweetened cocoa
 powder
½ cup buttermilk
2 eggs
1 teaspoon baking soda
1 teaspoon vanilla
 Very Cocoa Frosting

Prep: 30 minutes Bake: 22 minutes
Cool: 5 minutes Oven: 350°F
Nutrition facts per brownie: 191 cal.,
9 g fat, 27 mg chol., 98 mg sodium, 27 g carbo.,
0 g fiber, 2 g pro.

1. In a large mixing bowl, combine the flour and sugar.

2. In a medium heavy saucepan, combine the coffee, butter, shortening and cocoa powder. Heat to boiling, stirring constantly.

3. Pour boiling coffee mixture over flour and sugar in mixing bowl. Add the buttermilk, eggs, baking soda and vanilla. Beat with an electric mixer until combined.

4. Transfer batter to a greased 15×10×1-inch baking pan. Bake in a 350° oven for 22 to 25 minutes or until a toothpick inserted into center comes out clean. Cool in pan on a wire rack for 5 minutes.

5. Prepare Very Cocoa Frosting. Spread over warm brownies. Continue to cool on wire rack. Cut into bars.

Very Cocoa Frosting: In a medium saucepan, combine ½ cup butter or margarine, ¼ cup milk and 2 tablespoons unsweetened cocoa powder. Heat to boiling, stirring occasionally. Remove from heat. Add 3¾ cups sifted powdered sugar and 1 teaspoon vanilla. Beat with an electric mixer or wire whisk until smooth. Pour warm frosting over warm brownies and carefully spread frosting to edges.

Prairie Dunes
Cherry-Nut Ice Cream

MAKES 2 QUARTS (16 SERVINGS).

Prairie Dunes Country Club in Hutchinson, Kansas, the site of the 2002 U.S. Women's Open, was named for its windswept sandhills that challenge golfers. In the dining room, this extra-creamy cherry ice cream has been on the menu since 1994.

1   10-ounce jar red maraschino cherries
2   cups half-and-half or light cream
2   cups whipping cream
1   cup packed brown sugar
1   tablespoon vanilla
¾   cup chopped pecans, toasted
     Maraschino cherries (optional)
     Fresh mint leaves (optional)
     Shortbread cookies (optional)

Prep: 15 minutes Freeze: 25 minutes
Ripen: 4 hours
Nutrition facts per serving: 252 cal.,
18 g fat, 52 mg chol., 37 mg sodium,
22 g carbo., 1 g fiber, 2 g pro.

1. Drain cherries, reserving ⅓ cup juice. Chop cherries and set aside.

2. In a large bowl, combine the half-and-half, whipping cream, brown sugar, reserved cherry juice and vanilla. Stir until sugar is dissolved.

3. Spoon mixture into the freezer can of a 4- to 5-quart ice cream freezer. Freeze according to manufacturer's directions. Remove the dasher. Stir in the reserved maraschino cherries and pecans. Ripen ice cream according to the manufacturer's directions*. Garnish each serving with additional maraschino cherries with stems and fresh mint leaves, if you like. Serve with shortbread cookies, if you like.

*Note: Ripening ice cream improves the texture and helps to keep the ice cream from melting too quickly during eating. To ripen ice cream in a traditional-style ice cream freezer, after churning, remove the lid and dasher and cover the top of the freezer can with waxed paper or foil. Plug the hole in the lid with a small piece of cloth or paper towel; replace the lid. Pack the outer freezer bucket with enough ice and rock salt to reach the top of the freezer can (use 4 cups of ice to 1 cup of salt). Ripen about 4 hours.

Neapolitan Sundaes

"Angel food cake is a terrific low-fat dessert," says Rennee Schwartz, a fitness teacher and personal trainer at the Davenport Athletic Club in Davenport, Iowa. It's topped with summer strawberries and a touch of chocolate; you won't even miss the whipped cream.*

3	cups strawberries, hulled
4	slices angel food cake (about 1 ounce each)
1⅓	cups fat-free vanilla frozen yogurt
¼	cup miniature semisweet chocolate pieces, chopped semisweet chocolate, chopped milk chocolate and/or chopped white chocolate

Start to finish: 15 minutes
Nutrition facts per serving: 245 cal.,4 g fat, 0 mg chol., 175 mg sodium, 47 g carbo., 3 g fiber, 5 g pro.

1. Place 1 cup of the strawberries in a blender container or food processor bowl. Cover and blend or process until nearly smooth.

2. Slice the remaining strawberries. Drizzle strawberry puree evenly onto 4 dessert plates. Place cake slices on top of puree. Top each with ⅓ cup of the frozen yogurt. Sprinkle each with 1 tablespoon of the chocolate pieces. Top with the remaining strawberries. Serve immediately.

Fast and Easy Fudge Sauce

Vary the flavor of this delicious fudgy sauce by using espresso or different liqueurs. Try almond, hazelnut, or orange-flavored liqueur for a more grown-up taste. Paired with your favorite ice cream, the combinations are endless.

1 cup packed brown sugar

½ cup unsweetened cocoa powder

½ cup butter, cut up

½ cup whipping cream

2 teaspoons instant espresso or regular coffee granules or vanilla, or 2 tablespoons liqueur, such as amaretto (optional)

Start to finish: 20 minutes

Nutrition facts per 2-tablespoon serving:
175 cal., 11 g fat, 33 mg chol., 86 mg sodium, 18 g carbo., 0 g fiber, 1 g pro.

1. In a small bowl, combine brown sugar and cocoa powder; set aside. In a small heavy saucepan, melt butter in whipping cream over medium-low heat, stirring constantly. Cook and stir over medium heat for 5 to 6 minutes or until mixture just boils around edges.

2. Add the sugar-cocoa mixture to whipping cream mixture. Cook, stirring constantly, for 1 to 2 minutes more or until sugar is dissolved and mixture is thickened and smooth. Remove from heat; stir in espresso, vanilla or liqueur, if you like. Serve immediately on sundaes or with other desserts. Or cover and refrigerate for up to 1 week. Reheat in the microwave oven or on the range top.

Gathering everyone around the table

to experience the magic of the

season—that's the heart of the holiday.

From elegant nibbles to hearty roasts

Heart of the Holidays

and grand, glamorous party fare, here's a

selection of some of the best ways to

spread comfort and joy throughout

the season.

Sparkling Citrus-Sour Cream Sugar Cookies, page 178

Blueberry Surprise French Toast Casserole

MAKES 8 SERVINGS.

At Turkey Run Inn at Turkey Run State Park in east-central Indiana, guests look forward to the breakfast buffet that includes this enticing casserole. At home, assemble it the night before and have it ready to pop into the oven in the morning.

12 slices dry white bread, cut into ½-inch cubes (about 8 cups) *

2 8-ounce packages cream cheese, cut into ¾-inch cubes

1 cup fresh or frozen blueberries

12 eggs

2 cups milk

½ cup maple syrup or maple-flavored syrup

Blueberry-flavored, maple or maple-flavored syrup (optional)

Prep: 20 minutes Chill: 2 to 24 hours
Bake: 50 minutes Stand: 10 minutes
Oven: 375°F

Nutrition facts per serving without syrup:
503 cal., 30 g fat, 386 mg chol., 497 mg sodium, 40 g carbo., 1 g fiber, 19 g pro.

1. Place half of the bread cubes over the bottom of a well-buttered 13×9×2-inch baking dish (3-quart rectangular). Sprinkle cream cheese and blueberries over bread cubes. Arrange remaining bread cubes over blueberries.

2. In a large mixing bowl, beat eggs with a rotary beater; beat in milk and the ½ cup syrup. Carefully pour egg mixture over the bread mixture. Cover and chill in the refrigerator for 2 to 24 hours.

3. Bake, covered, in a 375° oven for 25 minutes. Uncover and bake about 25 minutes more or until a knife inserted near the center comes out clean and topping is puffed and golden brown. Let stand for 10 minutes before serving. Serve warm with blueberry-flavored or maple syrup, if you like.

*Note: To dry bread slices, arrange bread in a single layer on a wire rack; cover loosely and let stand overnight. Or cut bread into ½-inch cubes; spread in a large baking pan. Bake, uncovered, in a 300° oven for 10 to 15 minutes or until dry, stirring twice; cool.

Austrian Apple Pancakes

MAKES 6 TO 8 SERVINGS.

At The House on the Hill Bed and Breakfast in Ellsworth, Michigan, guests savor breakfast in a snow country setting. Although innkeepers Tom and Cindy Tomalka claim Polish descent, this Old World specialty is right at home on their table.

½   cup sugar
2   teaspoons ground cinnamon
3   tablespoons butter
3   medium Granny Smith and/or
    McIntosh apples, peeled,
    cored and thinly sliced
    (3 cups)
3   egg yolks
½   cup all-purpose flour
½   cup milk
¼   teaspoon salt
3   egg whites
    Whipped cream or dairy
    sour cream

Prep: 20 minutes Bake: 20 minutes Oven: 400°F
Nutrition facts per serving: 266 cal.,
12 g fat, 130 mg chol., 207 mg sodium,
36 g carbo., 2 g fiber, 5 g pro.

1. In a small bowl, combine the sugar and cinnamon. In a 10-inch ovenproof skillet, melt butter over medium-high heat; stir in sugar mixture until sugar is dissolved. Add apples and reduce heat. Cook and gently stir over medium heat for 3 minutes. Set aside.

2. In a medium mixing bowl, use a wire whisk to beat egg yolks slightly. Whisk in flour, milk and salt until combined. In a small mixing bowl, beat egg whites with an electric mixer until stiff peaks form (tips stand straight). Gently fold beaten egg whites into flour and egg yolk mixture, leaving a few fluffs of egg white. Do not over mix. Pour the batter over warm apple mixture in skillet, spreading evenly with a spatula.

3. Bake, uncovered, in a 400° oven about 20 minutes or until puffed and golden brown. Immediately loosen edge of pancake and turn upside down onto a heatproof 12-inch serving platter. If any apple slices stick to the bottom of the skillet, use a spatula to replace them on the pancake. (The pancake will fall after removing from the oven.) Cut into wedges. Top each serving with a small amount of whipped cream or sour cream.

Ravenwood's Beckoning Cinnamon Rolls

MAKES 12 ROLLS.

Talk about a crowd pleaser! Sue Maxwell, owner of Ravenwood Castle in New Plymouth, Ohio, calculates the kitchen has made about 15,000 of these glazed rolls in the past six years at her country inn. They're sure to be a hit with your crowd.

1	cup water
¼	cup butter, cut up
¼	cup granulated sugar
1	beaten egg
1	package active dry yeast
½	teaspoon salt
3½	to 4 cups all-purpose flour
¼	cup butter, softened
¾	cup packed brown sugar
2	teaspoons ground cinnamon
1	cup chopped nuts
	Powdered Sugar Icing

Prep: 35 minutes Rise 1½ hours Bake: 30 minutes
Oven: 350°F

Nutrition facts per roll: 400 cal., 18 g fat, 46 mg chol., 214 mg sodium, 56 g carbo., 2 g fiber, 6 g pro.

1. In a small saucepan, heat and stir water and the ¼ cup cut-up butter just until warm (105° to 115°) and butter almost melts. In a large mixing bowl, combine butter mixture, granulated sugar, egg, yeast and salt, stirring to dissolve yeast. Set aside for 10 minutes or until bubbly on top. Using a wooden spoon, stir in 2 cups of the flour; mix well. Stir in as much of the remaining flour as you can.

2. Turn dough out onto a floured surface. Knead in enough remaining flour to make a moderately soft dough that is smooth and elastic (3 to 5 minutes total). Shape dough into a ball. Place dough in a lightly greased bowl; turn once to grease surface of the dough. Cover and let rise in a warm place until double in size (about 1 hour).

3. Punch dough down. Turn dough onto a lightly floured surface. Cover dough and let rest 10 minutes. Grease a 13×9×2-inch baking pan; set aside. Roll dough into 18×10-inch rectangle. Spread with the ¼ cup softened butter. In a small bowl, combine brown sugar and cinnamon; sprinkle onto dough. Sprinkle with nuts. Tightly roll up into a spiral, starting from a long side. Pinch seams to seal.

4. Cut dough crosswise into 12 even slices. Arrange slices, cut sides down, in the prepared baking pan. Cover and let rise until nearly double (about 30 to 40 minutes) *.

5. Bake in a 350° oven about 30 minutes or until golden. Invert rolls onto a wire rack. Invert again onto serving platter. Cool slightly. Drizzle with Powdered Sugar Icing.

Powdered Sugar Icing: In a small bowl, combine 1 cup sifted powdered sugar, 2 tablespoons melted butter and ½ teaspoon vanilla. Stir in 2 tablespoons half-and-half or light cream, 1 teaspoon at a time, until icing reaches drizzling consistency.

*Note: If you like, omit the second rise: Cover shaped rolls loosely with plastic wrap; refrigerate overnight. Uncover rolls and let stand at room temperature for 20 minutes. Bake as above.

Twinkling Ginger Champagne Punch

MAKES 8 (4–OUNCE) SERVINGS.

This sparkling drink is a festive addition to the season's brunch at Tomfooleries Restaurant in Kansas City, Kansas. For a nonalcoholic option, prepare the gingered syrup without the vodka and use sparkling cider instead of the Champagne.

¼	cup sugar
¼	cup light-colored corn syrup
¼	cup water
3	tablespoons finely snipped crystallized ginger
½	cup vodka
1	750-ml bottle Champagne, chilled

Prep: 10 minutes Cook: 10 minutes Chill: 4 hours
Nutrition facts per serving: 150 cal., 0 g fat, 0 mg chol., 13 mg sodium, 16 g carbo., 0 g fiber, 0 g pro.

1. In a small saucepan, combine sugar, corn syrup, water and crystallized ginger. Bring to boiling; reduce heat. Simmer, uncovered, for 10 minutes. Remove from heat. Stir in vodka; cool to room temperature. Cover and chill in refrigerator for 4 hours or overnight. Strain the vodka mixture to remove the ginger; discard ginger.

2. Pour vodka mixture into a medium bowl. Slowly pour the Champagne down side of bowl; stir gently with an up-and-down motion to mix. To serve, ladle into punch cups. Serve immediately.

Michigan Smoked Whitefish Cakes

MAKES 7 APPETIZER OR 5 MAIN-DISH SERVINGS.

Move over, crab cakes! With a duo of Lake Michigan whitefish—both fresh and smoked—Stafford's Bay View Inn in Petoskey, Michigan, gives a Midwestern spin to the East Coast concept. Serve them as an appetizer or luncheon dish.

1 pound fresh, whole pan-dressed whitefish or trout, skinned
8 ounces smoked whitefish or trout, skinned and cut up
2 beaten eggs
½ cup fine dry bread crumbs
2 teaspoons dried dillweed
1 medium red and/or yellow sweet pepper, finely chopped (¾ cup)
1 stalk celery, finely chopped (½ cup)
1 green onion, finely sliced
3 tablespoons mayonnaise
¼ cup cooking oil
Sour Cream Dipping Sauce (optional)

Prep: 40 minutes Cook: 10 minutes/batch
Oven: 300°F
Nutrition facts per appetizer serving:
280 cal., 18 g fat, 111 mg chol., 571 mg sodium, 6 g carbo., 1 g fiber, 23 g pro.

1. Rinse fish; pat dry with paper towels. In a large skillet, bring ¼ inch of water to simmer. Add pan-dressed whitefish or trout. Simmer, covered, for 5 minutes or until fish flakes easily when tested with a fork. Remove from skillet and flake into small pieces (should have about 1½ cups). Discard cooking liquid.

2. In a food processor bowl or blender container, add smoked fish pieces. Cover and process or blend until finely chopped (should have about 1½ cups). Set aside.

3. In a large bowl, combine eggs, bread crumbs and dillweed. Stir in sweet pepper, celery, and green onion. Add flaked cooked fish, chopped smoked fish and mayonnaise; mix well. Using ¼ cup fish mixture for each cake, shape into fourteen ½-inch-thick patties (or for main dish-size cakes, use a ⅓-cup portion and shape into ten ½-inch-thick patties). Cover and refrigerate patties for up to 24 hours at this point, if you like.

4. In a large skillet, heat oil over medium heat. Add half of the patties. Cook, uncovered, over medium heat for 5 to 7 minutes per side or until golden brown. Drain on paper towels. Keep warm in a 300° oven while frying remaining patties. Serve warm with Sour Cream Dipping Sauce, if you like.

Sour Cream Dipping Sauce: In a small bowl, stir together ½ cup dairy sour cream, 1 teaspoon lemon juice and ¼ teaspoon dried dillweed.

Turkey-Cranberry Fingers

MAKES 16 APPETIZERS.

These appetizer-size turkey-cranberry sandwiches appear on the menu at the annual Tea with Scrooge held at the St. Paul Hotel. For a shortcut version, use purchased focaccia or another bread in place of the homemade herbed focaccia.

1¾ to 2¼ cups bread flour or all-purpose flour
1½ teaspoons active dry yeast
1½ teaspoons dried basil, crushed
1½ teaspoons dried thyme, crushed
½ teaspoon salt
½ teaspoon dried oregano, crushed
¾ cup warm water (120°F to 130°F)
1 tablespoon olive oil
1 12-ounce container cranberry-orange relish or 1 cup whole cranberry sauce
16 fresh watercress sprigs or spinach leaves
12 ounces very thinly sliced (shaved) cooked turkey
Fresh watercress sprigs (optional)

Prep: 30 minutes Rise: 65 minutes
Bake: 18 minutes Oven: 400°F
Nutrition facts per appetizer: 117 cal.,
1 g fat, 9 mg chol., 313 mg sodium, 21 g carbo.,
1 g fiber, 6 g pro.

1. For focaccia: In a large mixing bowl, combine 1 cup of the flour, the yeast, basil, thyme, salt and oregano. Add warm water and oil. Beat with an electric mixer on low speed for 30 seconds, scraping sides of bowl. Beat on high speed for 3 minutes. Stir in as much of the remaining flour as you can. Turn out onto a lightly floured surface. Knead in enough remaining flour to make a moderately stiff dough that is smooth and elastic (6 to 8 minutes total). Shape dough into a ball. Place in a lightly greased bowl; turn once to grease surface of dough. Cover and let rise in a warm place until double in size (about 45 minutes).

2. Punch dough down. Cover and let rest for 10 minutes. Lightly grease a 13×9×2-inch baking pan. Turn dough into prepared baking pan. With greased fingers, pat dough onto bottom of pan. Flour your hands. With two fingers, make ½-inch-deep indentations every 2 inches in the surface of the dough. Cover and let rise in a warm place until nearly double in size (20 to 30 minutes).

3. Bake in a 400° oven for 18 to 20 minutes or until light golden brown. Remove from baking pan; cool on a wire rack. Cut the focaccia into 16 equal rectangular pieces. Set aside.

4. To assemble sandwiches, split each focaccia rectangle in half horizontally. Spread about 1 tablespoon of cranberry relish on the cut side of each bottom piece of focaccia; top each with a watercress or spinach leaf. Tightly arrange about ½ to ¾ ounce of turkey on each; add the top piece of focaccia, cut side down. Trim filling, if necessary. If you like, garnish with additional watercress sprigs.

Onion-Dill Bread

MAKES 2 LOAVES (24 SERVINGS).

Whole wheat flour and a double dose of dill—dill seeds and fresh dill—combine in this earthy bread from Liz Clark of Keokuk, Iowa. Her secret to savoring its full fresh-baked glory? "Try a slice warm, just from the oven, with butter melting into it."

¼	cup warm water (105°F to 115°F)
1	package active dry yeast
1	teaspoon sugar
1	cup warm water (105°F to 115°F)
1½	teaspoons dillseed
1½	teaspoons sea salt or kosher salt
1	cup stone-ground whole wheat flour
2	to 2½ cups unbleached all-purpose flour or all-purpose flour
½	cup finely chopped onion
¼	cup snipped fresh dill

Prep: 40 minutes Rise: 1½ hours
Bake: 25 minutes Oven: 400°F

Nutrition facts per serving: 55 cal., 0 g fat, 0 mg chol., 101 mg sodium, 12 g carbo., 1 g fiber, 2 g pro.

1. In a large mixing bowl, combine the ¼ cup warm water, yeast and sugar. Let stand for 5 to 10 minutes or until yeast dissolves and mixture is bubbly on top.

2. Stir the remaining 1 cup warm water, dillseed and salt into the yeast mixture. Add whole wheat flour and mix well to combine. Add 1 cup of the all-purpose flour. Beat with an electric mixer on low speed for 30 seconds, scraping sides of bowl constantly. Beat on high speed for 3 minutes. Stir in onion, snipped dill and as much of the remaining all-purpose flour as you can with a wooden spoon.

3. Turn dough out onto a floured surface. Knead in enough remaining all-purpose flour to make a stiff dough that is smooth and elastic (8 to 10 minutes total). Shape dough into a ball. Place in a greased bowl; turn once to grease surface of dough. Cover and let rise in a warm place until double in size (about 1 hour).

4. Punch dough down. Turn dough out onto a lightly floured surface. Divide dough in half. Cover the dough and let rest for 10 minutes. Shape by gently pulling each portion into a ball, tucking edges beneath. Place loaves on a lightly greased large baking sheet. Flatten each dough round slightly to 5 inches in diameter. Cover and let rise in a warm place until nearly double in size (30 to 45 minutes). Using a sharp knife, make 3 or 4 cuts about ¼ inch deep across the top of each loaf.

5. Bake in a 400° oven for 25 to 30 minutes or until bread sounds hollow when lightly tapped. Cover loosely with foil during the last 5 to 10 minutes of baking to prevent overbrowning, if necessary. Immediately remove bread from baking sheet. Cool loaves on wire racks.

Pompe de Noël

MAKES 2 LOAVES (24 SERVINGS).

This bright, aromatic holiday bread, studded with citrus peel and flavored with orange flower water, hails from sun-drenched Provence in the South of France. Look for orange flower water at specialty baking shops or Asian markets. If you can't find it, omit it from the recipe.

¼ cup warm water (105°F to 115°F)
1 package active dry yeast
1 teaspoon sugar
1 cup warm water (105°F to 115°F)
¼ cup sugar
1 teaspoon salt
¼ cup olive oil
1 tablespoon orange flower water (optional)
1 teaspoon finely shredded orange peel
¼ cup stone-ground whole wheat flour
3¼ to 3¾ cups all-purpose flour
Cornmeal
All-purpose flour

Prep: 30 minutes Rise: 1¾ hours
Bake: 30 minutes Oven: 375°F
Nutrition facts per serving: 90 cal., 2 g fat, 0 mg chol., 98 mg sodium, 15 g carbo., 1 g fiber, 2 g pro.

1. In a large mixing bowl, combine the ¼ cup warm water, yeast and the 1 teaspoon sugar. Let stand for 5 to 10 minutes or until yeast dissolves and mixture is bubbly on top.

2. Stir the remaining 1 cup warm water, the ¼ cup sugar, salt, oil, orange flower water (if you like) and orange peel into the yeast mixture. Add whole wheat flour and mix well to combine. Let stand for 5 minutes. Add 1½ cups of the all-purpose flour. Beat with an electric mixer on low speed for 30 seconds, scraping sides of bowl constantly. Beat on high speed for 3 minutes, scraping sides of bowl occasionally. Stir in as much of the remaining all-purpose flour as you can with a wooden spoon.

3. Turn out onto a lightly floured surface. Knead in enough remaining flour to make a moderately soft dough that is smooth and elastic (3 to 5 minutes total). Shape dough into a ball. Place in a lightly greased bowl; turn once to grease surface of the dough. Cover and let rise in a warm place until double in size (about 1 hour).

4. Lightly grease a large baking sheet; sprinkle with cornmeal. Punch dough down. Turn dough out onto a lightly floured surface. Divide dough in half. Cover the dough and let rest for 10 minutes. Shape each half into a ball; flatten slightly to a 6-inch round loaf. Lightly coat tops with additional flour. Place loaves on the prepared baking sheet. Cover and let rise in a warm place until double in size (45 to 60 minutes). Using a sharp knife, make 3 or 4 cuts ¼ inch deep across top of each loaf.

5. Bake in a 375° oven about 30 minutes or until bread sounds hollow when lightly tapped. Cover loosely with foil during the last 5 to 10 minutes of baking to prevent overbrowning, if necessary. Immediately remove bread from baking sheet. Cool loaves on wire racks.

Dresden Stollen

MAKES 2 LOAVES (32 SERVINGS).

This classic German Christmas bread is traced back to the 1400s, and the Hotel Pattee in Perry, Iowa, keeps the beloved tradition alive. In their version, a variety of dried fruits and nuts dot the sweetly spiced oval-shaped egg bread.

½	cup dark rum or apple juice
⅓	cup finely snipped dried pineapple or apricots
⅔	cup golden and/or regular raisins
⅓	cup coarsely chopped dried tart red cherries
⅓	cup dried currants
5	to 5½ cups all-purpose flour
2	packages active dry yeast
¾	teaspoon ground cardamom
½	teaspoon ground cinnamon
⅛	teaspoon ground cloves
1	cup milk
½	cup butter
¼	cup granulated sugar
1	tablespoon honey
½	teaspoon salt
1	egg
½	cup chopped pecans
1	tablespoon butter, melted
	Vanilla Sugar or coarse sugar

Prep: 1 hour Rise: 2¾ hours Bake: 25 minutes
Oven: 350°F
Nutrition facts per serving: 162 cal., 5 g fat, 16 mg chol., 79 mg sodium, 24 g carbo., 1 g fiber, 3 g pro.

1. In a medium bowl, pour the rum over the pineapple, raisins, cherries, and currants. Set aside to soak, stirring occasionally.

2. In large mixing bowl, combine 2 cups of flour, the yeast, cardamom, cinnamon and cloves. In a medium saucepan, heat and stir milk, the ½ cup butter, the ¼ cup granulated sugar, honey and salt until warm (120° to 130°) and butter almost melts. Add to the flour mixture with the egg. Beat with an electric mixer on low speed for 30 seconds, scraping sides of bowl. Beat on high speed for 3 minutes. Stir in fruit-rum mixture, pecans and as much of the remaining flour as you can with a wooden spoon.

3. Turn out onto a floured surface. Knead in enough remaining flour to make a moderately soft dough that is smooth and elastic (3 to 5 minutes). Shape dough into a ball. Place in a greased bowl; turn once to grease surface of dough. Cover and let rise in a warm place until double in size (about 1¾ hours).

4. Grease 2 baking sheets; set aside. Punch dough down. Turn out onto a floured surface. Divide dough in half. Cover and let rest for 10 minutes. Form each half into a 9×4-inch loaf. Place on prepared baking sheets. Flatten slightly to form 11×7-inch ovals, slightly tapering ends. Without stretching, fold a long side over to within 1 inch of opposite side; press edges to seal. Cover; let rise until double in size (about 1 hour).

5. Bake in a 350° oven for 25 to 30 minutes or until bread sounds hollow when tapped. Cover loosely with foil during the last 10 minutes of baking to prevent overbrowning, if necessary. Transfer loaves to wire racks. Immediately brush with melted butter. While warm, sprinkle with Vanilla Sugar. Cool completely. Wrap and store in refrigerator at least overnight or for up to 2 days before serving.

Vanilla Sugar: In a small bowl, using your hands, rub ¼ teaspoon vanilla into 1 tablespoon granulated sugar. Stir in 1 tablespoon sifted powdered sugar. Spread mixture on a sheet of waxed paper to dry. When dry, crush the mixture slightly.

Herbed Winter Salad

MAKES 4 SERVINGS.

In winter, when homegrown tomatoes are a distant memory, take a tip from the kitchen of the Hotel Pattee in Perry, Iowa: Roasting plum tomatoes intensifies their flavor. Add fresh herbs, mushrooms, walnuts and grapes, and you'll have a festive, fresh salad.

6	cups mesclun (mixed baby greens) or torn mixed greens
4	plum tomatoes, halved lengthwise and seeded
1	tablespoon balsamic vinegar
¼	teaspoon salt
¼	teaspoon freshly ground black pepper
⅓	cup extra-virgin olive oil
2	tablespoons balsamic vinegar
1	teaspoon snipped fresh herb, such as basil, marjoram, oregano, rosemary, tarragon or thyme
¼	teaspoon salt
⅛	teaspoon freshly ground black pepper
1	cup sliced fresh crimini or button mushrooms
½	cup seedless red and/or green grapes, halved
¼	cup coarsely chopped walnuts, toasted

Prep: 20 minutes Roast: 20 minutes Oven: 425°F
Nutrition facts per serving: 269 cal., 24 g fat, 0 mg chol., 308 mg sodium, 14 g carbo., 3 g fiber, 4 g pro.

1. For salad greens: In a large bowl of cold water, immerse the salad greens. After a few minutes, lift out the greens. Immerse the greens again, if necessary, to remove any dirt or sand particles. Discard the water. Drain the greens in a colander.

2. Place the greens on a clean kitchen towel or several layers of paper towels; gently pat dry. (Or use a salad spinner to spin the greens dry.) Wrap dried greens in a dry kitchen towel or paper towels; refrigerate for at least 1 hour or up to several hours to crisp.

3. Line a small baking sheet with foil; lightly grease the foil. In a self-sealing plastic bag, combine tomatoes, the 1 tablespoon balsamic vinegar, the ¼ teaspoon salt and the ¼ teaspoon pepper. Seal and shake well to coat tomatoes with vinegar mixture. Arrange tomatoes, cut side down, on the prepared baking sheet. Roast in a 425° oven for 20 to 25 minutes or until tomato skins are bubbly and dark red but not burned. Set aside.

4. For vinaigrette: In a screw-top jar, combine oil, the 2 tablespoons vinegar, herb, the ¼ teaspoon salt and the ⅛ teaspoon pepper. Cover; shake well.

5. Arrange the mesclun on 4 chilled salad plates. Top with roasted tomatoes, mushrooms, grapes, and walnuts. Pour vinaigrette over salads. Serve immediately.

Grand Marnier Cranberry Relish

MAKES 10 TO 12 SERVINGS.

Keokuk cooking school proprietress Liz Clark bought her first food processor in 1973. The rest is history...and great recipes. Each holiday she was assigned the cranberry relish for the family feast, and this gussied up version calls on the ever-faithful kitchen tool.

1   pound cranberries (4 cups)
2   large seedless navel oranges, unpeeled and cut into 1-inch pieces
1   cup sugar
½   cup Grand Marnier liqueur or cranberry juice

Prep: 10 minutes Chill: 4 hours
Nutrition facts per serving: 141 cal., 0 g fat, 0 mg chol., 1 mg sodium, 31 g carbo., 2 g fiber, 0 g pro.

1. In a large food processor bowl fitted with a steel blade, place half of the cranberries and half of the oranges. Cover and process with several on-off pulses until fruit is finely chopped. Transfer to a large bowl. Repeat with remaining fruit. Add the sugar and liqueur or cranberry juice to the fruit mixture; stir to combine. Cover and chill for at least 4 hours or for up to 24 hours.

Potato-Corn Chowder in Bread Bowls

MAKES 8 SERVINGS.

For the Hometown Christmas celebration at the Hotel Pattee in Perry, Iowa, this comforting and creamy soup is ladled into bread bowls for a charming and rustic presentation. Consider serving it for a hearty and warming Christmas Eve soup supper.

1	16-ounce package frozen whole kernel corn
1	pound Yukon gold potatoes, peeled and cut into ½-inch cubes
2	tablespoons olive oil
½	cup thinly sliced leeks
2	tablespoons finely chopped shallots
4	cups chicken broth
1	teaspoon dried marjoram, crushed
½	teaspoon kosher salt or salt
½	teaspoon ground ginger
½	teaspoon ground white pepper
3	cups half-and-half or light cream
8	individual round loaves of sourdough bread
	Fresh marjoram sprigs (optional)

Prep: 25 minutes Roast: 20 minutes
Cook: 20 minutes Oven: 450°F
Nutrition facts per serving: 588 cal., 15 g fat, 33 mg chol., 1,221 mg sodium, 94 g carbo., 2 g fiber, 20 g pro.

1. Thaw frozen corn and pat dry with paper towels. Line a 15×10×1-inch baking pan with foil. Lightly grease the foil. Spread corn on half of the prepared pan. In a self-sealing plastic bag, combine potatoes and 1 tablespoon of the oil. Seal and shake well to coat potatoes with oil. Spread potatoes on the other half of the prepared pan. Roast, uncovered, in a 450° oven for 10 minutes; stir, keeping corn and potatoes separate. Continue to roast for 10 minutes more, stirring once or twice. Remove pan from oven. Set aside.

2. Transfer half of the roasted corn (about ¾ cup) to a food processor bowl or blender container. Cover and process or blend corn until pureed (if necessary, add a small amount of chicken broth to help mixture blend).

3. In a 4-quart Dutch oven, heat the remaining 1 tablespoon oil over medium-high heat. Add leeks and shallots. Reduce heat to medium. Cook and stir leek mixture for 6 to 8 minutes or until leeks are very soft and golden. Add whole kernel corn and pureed corn. Cook and stir for 1 minute. Stir in roasted potatoes, broth, dried marjoram, salt, ginger and white pepper. Bring to boiling; reduce heat. Simmer, covered, for 10 to 12 minutes or until potatoes are tender.

4. Add half-and-half. Cook and stir until heated through. Season to taste with additional salt and white pepper. Hollow out sourdough loaves. To serve, spoon chowder into bread bowls. Garnish with fresh marjoram sprigs, if you like.

Feast-Worthy Pecan and Sausage Stuffing

MAKES 10 TO 12 SERVINGS.

The holiday brunch spread at Tomfooleries Restaurant on Country Club Plaza in Kansas City, Missouri, wouldn't be complete without this fruit- and nut-studded cornbread stuffing. Try it alongside your holiday turkey this year.

1	pound bulk pork sausage
1½	cups chopped onion
1	cup chopped celery
2	beaten eggs
1	tablespoon ground sage
2	teaspoons poultry seasoning
1	teaspoon salt
½	teaspoon black pepper
4	cups crumbled corn bread
3	cups dry white bread cubes
2	cups finely chopped, peeled cooking apples
1	cup chopped pecans, toasted
½	cup snipped dried apricots
1½	cups chicken broth

Prep: 40 minutes Bake: 45 minutes Oven: 375°F
Nutrition facts per serving: 440 cal.,
27 g fat, 85 mg chol., 883 mg sodium,
38 g carbo., 3 g fiber, 12 g pro.

1. In a large skillet, cook sausage, onion and celery until meat is no longer pink. Do not drain; set aside.

2. In a very large bowl, combine the eggs, sage, poultry seasoning, salt and pepper. Add corn bread and white bread cubes; toss until coated. Add the cooked sausage mixture, apples, pecans and apricots. Add broth, tossing lightly to mix and moisten.

3. Place the stuffing in a lightly greased 3-quart casserole. Cover and bake in a 375° oven for 40 minutes. Uncover and bake 5 to 10 minutes more or until golden and an instant-read thermometer inserted near the center of stuffing registers 165°.

Praline Sweet Potatoes

MAKES 6 SERVINGS.

This dish appeared on last year's menu for *A Fireside Christmas performance at The Fireside, a dinner theater in Fort Atkinson, Wisconsin. You'll find it's an extra-festive way to serve sweet potatoes for a special holiday dinner.*

4	medium sweet potatoes or yams (1½ pounds)
½	to ¾ cup granulated sugar
¼	cup butter, melted
¼	teaspoon salt
½	cup evaporated milk
2	beaten eggs
¼	cup packed brown sugar
2	tablespoons all-purpose flour
1	tablespoon butter, melted
¼	cup chopped pecans

Prep: 45 minutes Bake: 30 minutes Oven: 350°F
Nutrition facts per serving: 365 cal., 17 g fat, 104 mg chol., 257 mg sodium, 50 g carbo., 3 g fiber, 6 g pro.

1. Wash and peel potatoes; cut into quarters. Cook potatoes in enough boiling, lightly salted water to cover for 25 to 30 minutes or until tender; drain well.

2. Grease a 2-quart square baking dish; set aside. In a large mixing bowl, beat sweet potatoes with an electric mixer on low speed until smooth. Beat in the granulated sugar, the ¼ cup melted butter and salt until well combined. Add milk and eggs. Beat just until combined. Spread the mixture evenly in the prepared baking dish.

3. For topping: In a small bowl, combine brown sugar, flour and the 1 tablespoon melted butter. Stir in pecans. Sprinkle topping over the sweet potato mixture. Bake in a 350° oven about 30 minutes or until set and topping is golden.

Roast Pork Loin with Dried Cherry and Wild Rice Stuffing

MAKES 8 TO 10 SERVINGS.

Michigan is known as cherry country, and the marshes of Minnesota yield an abundance of wild rice. This recipe pairs the two beloved ingredients for a show-stopping holiday entrée with a distinct regional flair.

⅓ cup wild rice

1 cup water

2 teaspoons snipped fresh rosemary

½ teaspoon salt

¾ cup coarsely chopped dried cherries or cranberries

1 3-pound boneless pork top loin roast (single loin)

6 ounces bulk pork sausage

½ cup chopped onion

1 tablespoon snipped fresh parsley

1 teaspoon snipped fresh thyme

¼ teaspoon freshly ground black pepper

1 cup water

⅓ cup cold water

2 tablespoons all-purpose flour
Salt and black pepper

Prep: 1 hour Cook: 40 minutes Roast: 1¼ hours
Stand: 15 minutes Oven: 325°F
Nutrition facts per serving: 377 cal., 15 g fat, 105 mg chol., 334 mg sodium, 17 g carbo., 1 g fiber, 41 g pro.

1. Rinse wild rice in a strainer under cold running water for 1 minute, lifting rice with your fingers to clean; drain. In a saucepan, combine rice, the 1 cup water, rosemary and the ½ teaspoon salt. Bring to boiling; reduce heat. Simmer, covered for 40 to 45 minutes or until rice is tender. Remove from heat. Stir in cherries. Set aside.

2. To butterfly roast, make a lengthwise cut down the center to within ½ inch of the opposite side. Spread open. At the center of each half, make a lengthwise cut parallel to the first cut, cutting to within ½ inch of opposite side. Cover roast with plastic wrap. Working from center to edges, pound with the flat side of a meat mallet to ½ to ¾ inch thick. Make sure the meat is of uniform thickness. Remove plastic wrap. Set aside.

3. For filling: In a large skillet, cook sausage and onion until sausage is brown and onion is tender. Drain fat. Stir in parsley, thyme and pepper. If necessary, drain cooked rice mixture to remove liquid. Stir cooked rice mixture into sausage mixture.

4. Spread filling over the surface of the butterflied roast. Roll loin up from a long side. Tie with kitchen string. (Wrap several strands of string crosswise around the meat and tie securely.) Place on a rack in a shallow roasting pan. Insert meat thermometer. Roast in a 325° oven for 1¼ to 1¾ hours or until thermometer registers 155°. Remove from oven. Cover loosely with foil; let stand for 15 minutes before carving. (The meat's temperature will rise 5° during standing.)

5. For pan gravy: Remove roast from roasting pan; cover to keep warm. Add 1 cup water to pan, scraping up browned bits. In a small saucepan, use a wire whisk to combine the ⅓ cup cold water and flour. Whisk in pan juices. Cook and stir over medium heat until thickened and bubbly. Cook and stir for 1 minute more. Season to taste with salt and black pepper.

6. Remove string from pork roast; discard. Slice roast. Arrange meat slices on a serving platter. Spoon pan gravy over the meat.

Choucroute Garnie with Cranberries

Makes 8 to 10 servings.

Midwesterners are blessed with a heritage of fine sausage making and have a long-standing love for the meat-and-potatoes style of eating. No wonder this hearty bistro dish from the Alsace region of France translates well.

1	tablespoon cooking oil
2	pounds pork loin back ribs, cut into serving-size pieces
1	pound smoked pork hocks
1	cup chopped onion
1½	pounds refrigerated sauerkraut, rinsed and drained
4	cups chicken broth
1½	cups dry white wine
1½	teaspoons dried thyme, crushed
2	bay leaves
1	teaspoon whole black peppercorns
½	teaspoon whole allspice
10	juniper berries
1	pound cooked smoked sausage, cut into 2-inch pieces
2	red cooking apples, cored and quartered
1½	cups cranberries
1	pound smoked pork chops
	Boiled Potatoes
	Assorted mustards

Prep: 15 minutes Cook: 1¼ hours
Nutrition facts per serving: 573 cal., 36 g fat, 114 mg chol., 2,433 mg sodium, 15 g carbo., 5 g fiber, 39 g pro.

1. In a 6-quart Dutch oven, heat the oil over medium heat. Add the ribs and cook until browned, turning occasionally. Remove and set aside. Add pork hocks and cook until browned, turning occasionally. Remove and set aside. Drain off all but 1 tablespoon fat. Add onion. Cook and stir until onion is tender. Return browned meat to the pan. Add sauerkraut, broth, wine and thyme. Bring to boiling. Place bay leaves, peppercorns, allspice, and juniper berries in the center of a 6-inch square of several layers of 100-percent-cotton cheesecloth. Bring the cheesecloth up around the spices. Using a cotton string, tie cheesecloth to form a bag. Trim excess cloth. Add to mixture in pan.

2. Reduce heat. Simmer, covered, for 45 minutes. Stir in smoked sausage, apples and cranberries. Place chops on top of mixture. Cover and cook 30 minutes more.

3. Remove pork hocks from Dutch oven; remove meat from bones and coarsely chop. Return chopped meat to pan (discard bones). Remove and discard spice bag. Using a slotted spoon, transfer all meat and sauerkraut to a large platter. Serve with Boiled Potatoes and assorted mustards.

Boiled Potatoes: Scrub 6 medium potatoes. Cut into 1½-inch pieces. Cook, covered, in lightly salted boiling water for 15 to 20 minutes or until tender. Drain. Season to taste with salt and pepper.

Morel-Bourbon Cream with Peppery Roast Beef

MAKES 8 TO 10 SERVINGS.

Pair succulent beef with an opulent morel-studded cream sauce and you'll have a spectacular entrée for your pull-out-all-the-stops holiday dinner party. For a colorful and easy accompaniment, consider serving with roasted vegetables.

1	2½- to 3-pound beef eye round roast
1	tablespoon cracked black pepper
1	ounce dried morel mushrooms
2	tablespoons unsalted butter
2	tablespoons finely chopped shallots
1	tablespoon all-purpose flour
½	cup beef broth
½	cup dry white wine
½	teaspoon ground ginger
¼	teaspoon salt
¼	teaspoon ground white pepper
1	cup whipping cream
2	tablespoons bourbon
	Salt and ground white pepper

Prep: 15 minutes Roast: 1½ hours
Stand 15 minutes Oven: 325°F
Nutrition facts per serving: 360 cal., 20 g fat, 111 mg chol., 241 mg sodium, 6 g carbo., 1 g fiber, 33 g pro.

1. For roast: Using the heel of your hand, gently press the cracked black pepper into the surface of the meat.

2. Place meat on a rack in a shallow roasting pan. Insert a meat thermometer. Roast in a 325° oven until thermometer registers 135° for medium rare * (1½ to 1¾ hours). Cover with foil; let stand 15 minutes before carving. (The meat's temperature will rise 10° during standing.)

3. Meanwhile, for sauce: In a small bowl, cover the dried mushrooms with hot water. Let stand 20 minutes. Drain and rinse mushrooms under warm running water; squeeze out excess moisture. Slice the mushrooms into rings. Set aside.

4. In a medium saucepan, melt butter over medium heat. Add the shallots. Cook and stir for 3 to 5 minutes or until shallots are tender. Stir in the flour. Add broth and wine. Bring to boiling. Simmer, uncovered, over medium-high heat for 6 to 8 minutes or until liquid has reduced by half, stirring often. Stir in ginger, the ¼ teaspoon salt and ¼ teaspoon white pepper. Whisk in the whipping cream. Cook, whisking constantly, over medium heat for 5 minutes or until mixture thickens. Stir in the reserved mushrooms and bourbon. Cook and stir until heated through. Season to taste with additional salt and ground white pepper.

5. To serve, thinly slice meat across the grain. Arrange meat slices on a serving platter. Pour some sauce over the meat. Pass remaining sauce.

*Note: Roasting past medium rare is not recommended.

Porcini-Herb Crusted Roast Rack of Lamb

MAKES 4 SERVINGS.

Lamb rib roast—known as rack of lamb in restaurant lingo—makes an impressive holiday entrée, especially when you serve it with Tuscan-inspired White Bean Ragoût (see recipe, page 176). For an excellent wine choice, try a full-bodied Côtes du Rhône.

2   6-rib lamb rib roasts (2 to 2½ pounds each), with or without backbone
1   ounce dried porcini mushrooms
1   teaspoon kosher salt
1   teaspoon freshly ground black pepper
¼   cup olive oil
2   tablespoons Worcestershire sauce
3   large shallots
4   cloves garlic
2   tablespoons snipped fresh thyme
2   tablespoons snipped fresh rosemary
    White Bean Ragoût (page 176)
    Fresh rosemary sprigs (optional)
    Chopped chives (optional)

Prep: 25 minutes Chill: Several hours
Roast: 1 hour Stand: 15 minutes Oven: 325°F
Nutrition facts per serving: 328 cal., 22 g fat, 64 mg chol., 623 mg sodium, 12 g carbo., 1 g fiber, 21 g pro.

1. Trim fat from meat. Set aside.

2. For porcini-herb crust: In a food processor bowl with a metal blade, combine dried mushrooms, salt and black pepper. Cover and process mushrooms to a powder. Add oil, Worcestershire sauce, shallots and garlic. Cover and process mixture until pureed. Stir in thyme and 2 tablespoons rosemary. Using your fingers, gently press the porcini-herb mixture onto all meaty sides of lamb. Cover and refrigerate for several hours or overnight.

3. Remove lamb from refrigerator. Place lamb, meaty side up, on a rack in a shallow roasting pan. Roast in a 325° oven until an instant-read thermometer inserted in a meaty portion of lamb registers 140° for medium rare (1 to 1¼ hours). Transfer lamb to a cutting board. Cover loosely with foil; let stand 15 minutes before carving. (The meat's temperature will rise 5° during standing.)

4. To carve lamb, cut into chops by slicing between rib bones. To serve, evenly divide the White Bean Ragoût among 4 shallow soup plates. Arrange the chops around the beans. Garnish with rosemary sprigs and chopped chives, if you like.

White Bean Ragoût

MAKES 4 SIDE-DISH SERVINGS.

With its bevy of culinary treasures, including flavorful prosciutto, earthy porcini mushrooms and robust Swiss chard, this Tuscan-style recipe produces memorable results with great ingredients rather than complicated techniques.

¾ cup dry cannellini (white kidney) beans or Great Northern beans

3 cups cold water

1 14-ounce can beef broth

½ ounce dried porcini mushrooms (⅓ cup)

6 ounces Swiss chard

1 tablespoon olive oil

2 tablespoons chopped shallots

2 cloves garlic, minced

1 ounce prosciutto or fully cooked ham, cut into thin strips (about 3 tablespoons)

2 or 3 sprigs fresh thyme

½ cup water

¼ cup dry red wine

2 plum tomatoes, peeled, seeded and chopped

2 tablespoons snipped fresh Italian parsley
Salt and freshly ground black pepper

Prep: 2 hours Cook: 22 minutes
Nutrition facts per serving: 212 cal., 5 g fat, 5 mg chol., 595 mg sodium, 29 g carbo., 8 g fiber, 13 g pro.

1. Rinse beans. In a large bowl, cover the beans with the 3 cups cold water. Let soak in a cool place for 8 hours or overnight; drain and rinse beans. (Or in a large saucepan, combine beans and cold water. Bring to boiling; reduce heat. Simmer for 2 minutes. Remove from heat. Cover and let soak for 1 hour; drain and rinse beans.)

2. In a medium saucepan, combine the soaked beans and beef broth. Bring to boiling; reduce heat. Simmer, covered, for 1 to 1¼ hours or until beans are tender. Drain the beans, reserving 1 cup of the beef broth. (If necessary, add additional broth or water to equal 1 cup.) Set beans and broth aside.

3. Meanwhile, in a small bowl, combine dried porcini mushrooms and hot water. Let soak in a cool place for 1 hour. Drain and rinse mushrooms under warm running water; squeeze out excess moisture. Set aside.

4. Thoroughly wash the chard under cold running water; drain well. Cut off the stalks at the base of the leaves. Cut the stalks into 1-inch pieces. Cut out the heavy center vein in the leaves; discard. Stack the leaves and cut into thin shreds; set aside.

5. In a large saucepan, heat the oil over medium heat. Add shallots and garlic. Cook and stir over medium heat for 3 minutes. Add drained mushrooms, prosciutto and thyme sprigs. Cook and stir for 3 minutes more. Add the reserved beef broth, the ½ cup water and the red wine. Bring to boiling; reduce heat. Simmer, uncovered, over medium-high heat for 10 to 15 minutes or until liquid is reduced by half, stirring often. Reduce heat to medium. Stir in reserved beans, Swiss chard pieces and tomatoes. Cook for 5 minutes more, stirring occasionally. Stir in chard leaf shreds and parsley. Cook and stir for 1 to 2 minutes more or just until leaves start to wilt. Season to taste with salt and black pepper. Remove thyme sprigs; discard. If you like, serve with Porcini-Herb Crusted Roast Rack of Lamb (page 174).

Lemon-Rosemary Roast Chicken

MAKES 6 SERVINGS.

If the holiday finds you hosting a smaller crowd this year, consider serving these easy marinate-and-roast chicken breasts. You'll still fill your home with the aroma and anticipation of a succulent roasted bird, but in less time and with less hassle.

6	large chicken breast halves (about 4½ pounds total)
1	cup lemon juice
¼	cup olive oil
2	tablespoons honey
2	tablespoons Dijon-style mustard
1	tablespoon snipped fresh rosemary or 1 teaspoon dried rosemary, crushed
2	cloves garlic, minced
¼	teaspoon salt
¼	teaspoon freshly ground black pepper

Prep: 15 minutes Marinate: 2 hours
Roast: 25 minutes   Oven: 425°F
Nutrition facts per serving: 490 cal.,
26 g fat, 173 mg chol., 195 mg sodium,
3 g carbo., 0 g fiber, 57 g pro.

1. Place chicken breasts in a large self-sealing plastic bag set in a shallow dish.

2. For marinade: In a small bowl, combine lemon juice, oil, honey, mustard, rosemary, garlic, salt and black pepper. Pour the marinade over chicken. Close bag. Marinate in the refrigerator for 2 to 4 hours, turning occasionally.

3. Drain chicken, discarding marinade. Place chicken, skin side up, in a shallow roasting pan. Roast, uncovered, in a 425° oven for 25 to 30 minutes or until chicken is golden brown and an instant-read thermometer inserted in chicken registers 170°.

Sparkling Citrus–Sour Cream Sugar Cookies

MAKES 40 TO 50 COOKIES.

With a spark of citrus gleaned from lemon extract and orange peel, these cookies will stand out on your holiday cookie tray. Top them with Powdered Sugar Glaze or your favorite frosting or add sprinkles to the cutouts before baking.

½	cup butter, softened
1	cup granulated sugar
1	teaspoon baking powder
¼	teaspoon baking soda
	Dash salt
½	cup dairy sour cream
1	egg
½	teaspoon lemon extract
1	teaspoon finely shredded orange peel
2½	cups all-purpose flour
	Powdered Sugar Glaze or your favorite frosting
	Edible glitter or other cookie decorations or sifted powdered sugar

Prep: 30 minutes Chill: 1 hour
Bake: 6 minutes/batch Oven: 375°F
Nutrition facts per cookie: 96 cal., 3 g fat, 13 mg chol., 50 mg sodium, 16 g carbo., 0 g fiber, 1 g pro.

1. In a large mixing bowl, beat butter with an electric mixer on medium to high speed for 30 seconds. Add granulated sugar, baking powder, baking soda and salt; beat until well combined. Beat in the sour cream, egg, lemon extract and orange peel.

2. Beat in as much flour as you can with the mixer. Using a wooden spoon, stir in remaining flour. Divide dough in half. Cover and chill for 1 to 2 hours or until dough is easy to handle.

3. On a well-floured surface, roll half of the dough at a time to ¼ inch thick. Using cookie cutters of various sizes, cut into desired shapes. Place cookies 1 inch apart on an ungreased cookie sheet.

4. Bake in a 375° oven for 6 to 7 minutes or until edges are firm and bottoms are light brown. Transfer cookies to a wire rack to cool.

5. Prepare Powdered Sugar Glaze or frosting. Spread cookies with glaze and sprinkle with edible glitter or other decorations, if you like. Or omit glaze and sprinkle warm cookies with powdered sugar.

Powdered Sugar Glaze: In a medium bowl, combine 4 cups sifted powdered sugar and ¼ cup milk. Stir in additional milk, 1 teaspoon at a time, until glaze reaches drizzling consistency.

Honey and Dried Cranberry Gingerbread

MAKES 12 SERVINGS.

For this recipe, Liz Clark, owner of a cooking school in Keokuk, Iowa, calls on honey instead of molasses, making a lighter-flavored gingerbread. Yet with true-to-tradition spices, the results are as homey and warming as ever. Bake a pan on a chilly winter day and you'll see.

2½	cups all-purpose flour
½	cup sugar
1	teaspoon baking powder
1	teaspoon baking soda
1	teaspoon ground ginger
½	teaspoon salt
½	teaspoon ground cinnamon
½	teaspoon ground mace or ground nutmeg
⅛	teaspoon ground cloves
2	beaten eggs
½	cup buttermilk
¾	cup honey
½	cup butter or shortening, melted and cooled
½	cup dried cranberries (coarsely chopped, if you like)
	Whipped cream (optional)

Prep: 20 minutes Bake: 45 minutes
Cool: 20 minutes Oven: 350°F
Nutrition facts per serving: 294 cal., 9 g fat, 58 mg chol., 341 mg sodium, 50 g carbo., 1 g fiber, 4 g pro.

1. Grease and flour a 2-quart rectangular baking dish. Set aside.

2. In a large bowl, combine flour, sugar, baking powder, baking soda, ginger, salt, cinnamon, mace and cloves. In a medium bowl, combine eggs, buttermilk, honey and butter.

3. Stir the buttermilk mixture into flour mixture with a wooden spoon, stirring just until combined. Fold in cranberries. Pour batter into prepared pan.

4. Bake in a 350° oven for 45 to 50 minutes or until a wooden toothpick inserted near the center comes out clean. Cool for 20 to 30 minutes on a wire rack. Serve warm with whipped cream, if you like.

Something Special Apple-Cherry Pie

MAKES 8 SERVINGS.

This recipe combines everyone's favorite pie fillings—apple and cherry—into one marvelous pie. A layer of toasted almonds adds a nutty crunch that makes the dessert holiday special—especially if you top it all off with a scoop of vanilla bean ice cream.

Pastry for a Double-Crust Pie (page 142)

- ½ cup almonds, toasted and chopped
- 6 cups thinly sliced, peeled Jonathan or Golden Delicious apples
- ⅓ cup cherry preserves
- ½ cup sugar
- 3 tablespoons all-purpose flour
- ½ teaspoon ground cardamom
- 1 cup frozen unsweetened pitted tart red cherries, thawed
  Milk
  Sugar

Prep: 25 minutes Bake: 55 minutes Oven: 375°F
Nutrition facts per serving: 481 cal., 22 g fat, 0 mg chol., 225 mg sodium, 68 g carbo., 4 g fiber, 6 g pro.

1. Prepare Pastry for Double-Crust Pie. On a lightly floured surface, slightly flatten one of the dough balls. Roll from center to edges to form a 12-inch circle. Wrap pastry circle around a rolling pin; unroll into a 9-inch pie plate. Trim bottom pastry to ½ inch beyond edge of pie plate. Sprinkle the toasted almonds on the bottom crust.

2. In a large bowl, toss apples with cherry preserves. In a small bowl, stir together the ½ cup sugar, flour and cardamom. Add to the apple mixture; add cherries. Gently toss to coat.

3. Transfer mixture to the pastry-lined pie plate. Roll out remaining pastry and cut into ½-inch-wide strips. (Use a fluted pastry wheel to cut strips, if you like.) Weave strips over filling for a lattice crust. Press ends of strips into crust rim. Fold bottom pastry over strips; seal and crimp edge. Brush with milk and sprinkle with additional sugar.

4. To prevent overbrowning, cover edge of pie with a metal piecrust shield or foil. Bake in a 375° oven for 25 minutes. Remove shield or foil. Bake for 30 to 35 minutes more or until top is golden and filling is bubbly in center of pie. Cool on a wire rack.

Eggnog Cheesecake with Cashew Crust

MAKES 16 SERVINGS.

Around the holidays, who can resist featuring eggnog in delicious dessert recipes from cookies to crème brûlée? Here, in a new variation on the theme, the beloved holiday beverage adds creaminess to this luscious cheesecake with an irresistible cashew crust.

1	cup finely ground cashews
1	cup finely crushed graham crackers (14 squares)
½	cup sugar
½	cup butter, melted
4	8-ounce packages cream cheese, softened
1	cup sugar
1	tablespoon rum (optional)
1	teaspoon vanilla
½	teaspoon ground nutmeg
3	eggs
1½	cups dairy eggnog
	Broken nut brittle (optional)

Prep: 20 minutes Bake: 1 hour Cool: 2 hours
Chill: 24 hours Oven: 350°F
Nutrition facts per serving: 450 cal.,
34 g fat, 118 mg chol., 288 mg sodium,
31 g carbo., 0 g fiber, 8 g pro.

1. For crust: In a medium bowl, stir together ground cashews, crushed graham crackers and the ½ cup sugar. Drizzle the melted butter over the cashew mixture. Toss until mixed well. Press the cashew mixture onto the bottom and about 1½ inches up the sides of a 10-inch springform pan. Wrap outside of the springform pan securely with heavy foil. Set aside.

2. For filling: In a large mixing bowl, beat the cream cheese with an electric mixer on medium-high speed for 3 to 4 minutes or until light and fluffy. Gradually beat in the 1 cup sugar for 2 to 3 minutes or until mixture is completely smooth, scraping sides of bowl. Reduce speed to medium; beat in rum (if you like), vanilla and nutmeg. Add eggs all at once; beat on low speed just until combined. Stir in eggnog.

3. Pour filling into crust-lined pan. Place springform pan in a large roasting pan*. (Make sure there is at least 1 inch between springform pan and edges of roasting pan.) Place roasting pan on oven rack. Carefully pour enough hot tap water into roasting pan to come halfway up sides of springform pan.

4. Bake in a 350° oven for 60 to 70 minutes or until edge of cheesecake is firm and center appears nearly set when lightly shaken. Carefully remove cheesecake pan from water bath; transfer to a wire rack and cool for 15 minutes. Remove foil. Loosen crust from sides of pan and cool 30 minutes more. Remove sides of pan and cool completely. Cover cheesecake with plastic wrap and refrigerate overnight. (Or store in refrigerator for up to 2 days.) To serve, cut into wedges and sprinkle each piece with nut brittle, if you like.

*Note: To bake cheesecake without a water bath, prepare cheesecake as above, except omit wrapping pan with foil. Place springform pan with filling in a shallow baking pan. Bake without water bath for 45 to 50 minutes or until center appears nearly set when shaken. The cheesecake's surface will have a more golden color.

Cranberry Chocolate Layer Cake

MAKES 12 TO 16 SERVINGS.

Layer cakes are a Midwestern church-social favorite. This comforting dessert gets a gourmet and glamorous touch with a sprinkling of cranberries and a luscious Chocolate Buttercream frosting.

1	tablespoon unsweetened cocoa powder
1¾	cups sifted cake flour
1	cup unsweetened cocoa powder
2	teaspoons baking soda
½	teaspoon salt
½	cup unsalted butter, softened
2	cups sugar
2	teaspoons vanilla
2	eggs
1¾	cups buttermilk (or 1¼ cups milk and ½ cup dairy sour cream)
¼	cup strong brewed coffee
½	cup dried cranberries or coarsely chopped dried tart red cherries
½	cup cranberry or red currant jelly, or loganberry or seedless red raspberry jam Chocolate Buttercream

Prep: 25 minutes Bake: 30 minutes Oven: 350°F
Nutrition facts per serving: 444 cal., 24 g fat, 78 mg chol., 279 mg sodium, 53 g carbo., 1 g fiber, 6 g pro.

1. Butter two 9-inch round baking pans. Add 1 tablespoon cocoa powder to one pan. Tilt and roll pan to coat with cocoa; shake out excess cocoa into second pan. Repeat to coat bottom and sides of second pan. Shake out excess cocoa; set aside.

2. In a medium bowl, stir together the cake flour, 1 cup cocoa powder, baking soda and salt. Set aside. In a large mixing bowl, beat ½ cup butter with an electric mixer on medium to high speed for 30 seconds. Add sugar and vanilla; beat until well combined. Add eggs, one at a time, beating well after each addition. In a small bowl, stir together the buttermilk and coffee. Add flour mixture and buttermilk mixture alternately to butter mixture, beating on low speed after each addition just until combined. Fold in cranberries. Divide batter evenly between prepared pans.

3. Bake in a 350° oven for 30 to 35 minutes or until a wooden toothpick inserted near the centers comes out clean. Cool cakes in pans on wire racks for 10 minutes. Remove cakes from pans. Cool thoroughly on wire racks before frosting.

4. Place one cake layer on a serving plate. With a thin metal spatula, spread the jelly or jam on the cake to within ½ inch of the edges. Top with a layer of Chocolate Buttercream (about ⅓ cup). Place second cake layer on top. Frost the top and sides with Chocolate Buttercream. Chill in refrigerator to firm buttercream.

Chocolate Buttercream: In a small saucepan, melt 5 ounces semisweet chocolate and 1 ounce unsweetened chocolate over low heat. Cool to room temperature. In a food processor bowl with a metal blade, combine cooled chocolate and ¼ cup sugar, if you like. Add ¼ cup refrigerated or frozen egg product, thawed, 1 to 2 tablespoons instant espresso coffee powder, 1 tablespoon cognac or orange liqueur and 1 teaspoon vanilla. Cover and process with 4 to 5 on/off turns to mix. With machine running, add 1 cup unsalted butter, cut up, one piece at a time, through feed tube. Process until smooth. If necessary, chill until it reaches spreading consistency.

Peppermint Fudge

MAKES ABOUT 4 POUNDS (96 PIECES).

Fudge is prettied up in holiday hues thanks to a quick sprinkling of broken peppermint candies. If you like, use 2 cups mint-flavored semisweet chocolate pieces instead of the semisweet chocolate and the peppermint extract.

4   cups sugar

2   5-ounce cans (1⅓ cups total) evaporated milk

1   cup butter

1   12-ounce package (2 cups) semisweet chocolate pieces

1   7-ounce jar marshmallow creme

½   teaspoon peppermint extract

¾   cup coarsely broken peppermint candies

Prep: 20 minutes Cook: 10 minutes

Nutrition facts per piece of fudge: 83 cal., 3 g fat, 6 mg chol., 26 mg sodium, 14 g carbo., 0 g fiber, 0 g pro.

1. Line a 13×9×2-inch pan with foil, extending foil over edges of pan. Butter foil and set pan aside.

2. Butter the sides of a heavy 3-quart saucepan. In the saucepan, combine sugar, evaporated milk and the 1 cup butter. Cook and stir over medium-high heat until mixture boils. Reduce heat to medium; cook and stir for 10 minutes more.

3. Remove pan from heat. Add chocolate pieces, marshmallow creme and peppermint extract. Stir until chocolate melts and mixture is combined. Using a wooden spoon, beat by hand for 1 minute. Spread into prepared pan. Sprinkle with peppermint candies. Score into 1-inch pieces while warm. Cover and chill.

4. When fudge is firm, use foil to lift candy out of the pan. Cut into squares. Store in tightly covered container in the refrigerator.

Test Kitchen Tip: To coarsely break the peppermint candies, place them in a self-sealing plastic bag. Seal bag. Using a rolling pin, break candies into pieces. Put broken candies in a sieve to separate the larger pieces from the fine particles.

Index

Photographs indicted in bold.

Metric Information

The charts on this page provide a guide for converting measurements from the U.S. customary system, which is used throughout this book, to the metric system.

Product Differences

Most of the ingredients called for in the recipes in this book are available in most countries. However, some are known by different names. Here are some common American ingredients and their possible counterparts:

- Sugar (white) is granulated, fine granulated, or castor sugar.
- Powdered sugar is icing sugar.
- All-purpose flour is enriched, bleached or unbleached white household flour. When self-rising flour is used in place of all-purpose flour in a recipe that calls for leavening, omit the leavening agent (baking soda or baking powder) and salt.
- Light-colored corn syrup is golden syrup.
- Cornstarch is cornflour.
- Baking soda is bicarbonate of soda.
- Vanilla or vanilla extract is vanilla essence.
- Green, red, or yellow sweet peppers are capsicums or bell peppers.
- Golden raisins are sultanas.

Volume and Weight

The United States traditionally uses cup measures for liquid and solid ingredients. The chart below shows the approximate imperial and metric equivalents. If you are accustomed to weighing solid ingredients, the following approximate equivalents will be helpful.

- 1 cup butter, castor sugar, or rice = 8 ounces = ½ pound = 250 grams
- 1 cup flour = 4 ounces = ¼ pound = 125 grams
- 1 cup icing sugar = 5 ounces = 150 grams

Canadian and U.S. volume for a cup measure is 8 fluid ounces (237 ml), but the standard metric equivalent is 250 ml.

1 British imperial cup is 10 fluid ounces.

In Australia, 1 tablespoon equals 20 ml, and there are 4 teaspoons in the Australian tablespoon.

Spoon measures are used for smaller amounts of ingredients. Although the size of the tablespoon varies slightly in different countries, for practical purposes and for recipes in this book, a straight substitution is all that's necessary. Measurements made using cups or spoons always should be level unless stated otherwise.

Common Weight Range Replacements

Imperial / U.S.	Metric
½ ounce	15 g
1 ounce	25 g or 30 g
4 ounces (¼ pound)	115 g or 125 g
8 ounces (½ pound)	225 g or 250 g
16 ounces (1 pound)	450 g or 500 g
1¼ pounds	625 g
1½ pounds	750 g
2 pounds or 2¼ pounds	1,000 g or 1 Kg

Oven Temperature Equivalents

Fahrenheit Setting	Celsius Setting*	Gas Setting
300°F	150°C	Gas Mark 2 (very low)
325°F	160°C	Gas Mark 3 (low)
350°F	180°C	Gas Mark 4 (moderate)
375°F	190°C	Gas Mark 5 (moderate)
400°F	200°C	Gas Mark 6 (hot)
425°F	220°C	Gas Mark 7 (hot)
450°F	230°C	Gas Mark 8 (very hot)
475°F	240°C	Gas Mark 9 (very hot)
500°F	260°C	Gas Mark 10 (extremely hot)
Broil	Broil	Grill

*Electric and gas ovens may be calibrated using celsius. However, for an electric oven, increase celsius setting 10 to 20 degrees when cooking above 160°C. For convection or forced air ovens (gas or electric) lower the temperature setting 25°F/10°C when cooking at all heat levels.

Baking Pan Sizes

Imperial / U.S.	Metric
9×1½-inch round cake pan	22- or 23×4-cm (1.5 L)
9×1½-inch pie plate	22- or 23×4-cm (1 L)
8×8×2-inch square cake pan	20×5-cm (2 L)
9×9×2-inch square cake pan	22- or 23×4.5-cm (2.5 L)
11×7×1½-inch baking pan	28×17×4-cm (2 L)
2-quart rectangular baking pan	30×19v4.5-cm (3 L)
13×9×2-inch baking pan	34×22×4.5-cm (3.5 L)
15×10×1-inch jelly roll pan	40×25×2-cm
9×5×3-inch loaf pan	23×13×8-cm (2 L)
2-quart casserole	2 L

U.S. / Standard Metric Equivalents

⅛ teaspoon = 0.5 ml

¼ teaspoon = 1 ml

½ teaspoon = 2 ml

1 teaspoon = 5 ml

1 tablespoon = 15 ml

2 tablespoons = 25 ml

¼ cup = 2 fluid ounces = 50 ml

⅓ cup = 3 fluid ounces = 75 ml

½ cup = 4 fluid ounces = 125 ml

⅔ cup = 5 fluid ounces = 150 ml

¾ cup = 6 fluid ounces = 175 ml

1 cup = 8 fluid ounces = 250 ml

2 cups = 1 pint = 500 ml

1 quart = 1 litre